THE TREE OF LIFE

THE TREE
OF LIFE

HUGH NISSENSON

1817

HARPER & ROW, PUBLISHERS, New York
Cambridge, Philadelphia, San Francisco, London
Mexico City, São Paulo, Singapore, Sydney

Designer: Sidney Feinberg

Library of Congress Cataloging in Publication Data

Nissenson, Hugh.
   The tree of life.
      1. Ohio—History—1787–1865—Fiction.   2. Appleseed,
Johnny, 1774–1845—Fiction.   I. Title.
PS3564.I8T7   1985   813'.54   84-48615
ISBN 0-06-015143-9

For Marilyn, Kate, and Kore, and for Don Hutslar,
without whom I could neither have written
nor illustrated this novel

THE TREE OF LIFE

The Gods of the earth and sea
Sought through nature to find this Tree;
But their search was all in vain:
There grows one in the Human brain.
        —WILLIAM BLAKE, "The Human Abstract"

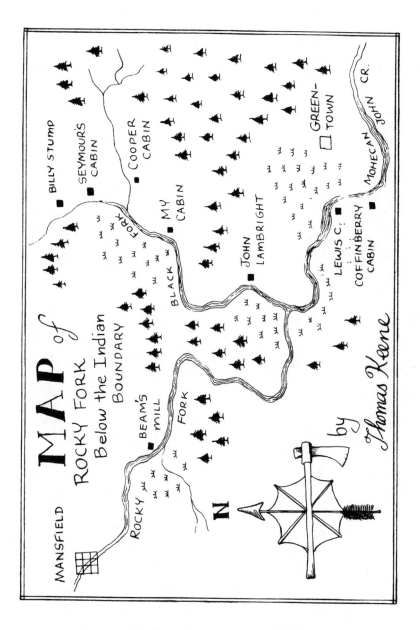

Courtesy of the Thomas Keene Collection, Mansfield, Ohio.

At the NW. Bend of the Black Fork of Mohecan John's Creek, Richland County, Ohio

1811

An inventory of my Business, owing to & by me, Thomas Keene, taken this Day; & is as follows, viz.

1 July.
Imprimis.

I have in ready cash	$17.62.

Item.

1 middle horned red Devon working & milch cow, Juno, 5 yrs. old, a light dun ring round the left eye	30.00.
1 calf's stomach, preserved by salt	.20.
1 U.S. Model Harpers Ferry rifle, carrying a ball of 30 per lb.	15.00.
1 hammered copper Still, well-tinned, of 27½ gall.	14.30.
1 hammered copper Head, with pewter charging pipe, etc.	4.30.
1 set of maple Worm tubs, hickory hoops	.90.
2 vials for testing whisky's proof	.30.
6 bushels of malt	.30.

I am indebted as follows,

To the Federal Government's Land Office, Canton, Ohio, for 160 prime acres, T21, R18, $320.00, for which on 30 September, 1810, I paid down $16.00, the first installment. Deferred to pay till 30 Sept., 1813	$304.00.

1 July.

Bought of Levi Jones at his store in Mansfield,
1 Ledger, bound in calf skin, for this Waste
Book.. .50.
Bought of the above, 3 steel pens @ .01 .... .03.
Ditto, the above, 2 sticks, India ink, @ .11 .... .22.
Sold to Isaac Williams at his Tavern in
Mansfield, 9 lbs. cheese..................................... .58.
The balance due me to be paid there, the 4th
Instant, by 9 AM, or before roll call at General
Muster, in 1 gall. whisky.

4 July.

Received in full at 6 AM from Isaac Williams,
the above.

Atop the white oak stump in Central Park, Mansfield, John
Chapman read the Declaration of Independence aloud.

The Rev. Cooper, in his Sunday best, led us in a special
prayer for continuing peace in the Territory. He also said,

"Thanks be to God, there are now 26 of us hereabouts.
An increase of 8 since last July 4th: Brother Lewis and his
family, come from Buffalo, New York State; George and
Delight Coffinberry, and their three fine boys, here from
Shenandoah County, Va., to join his brother, Bob; and
Brother Keene, lately of Lancaster County, Pennsylvania.
Welcome!"

Old man Seymour was elected Orderly Sergeant. Beam
played "Yankee Doodle," on his fife, accompanied on the
drum by Bob Coffinberry. We fired a volley in the air.

The Rev. took his family home. Mrs. Cooper and Sarah
mounted their roan mare, Liz. Henry and Fanny walked
behind. She was wearing a new calico bodice—pale blue like
her eyes. He held her hand.

I joined the crowd at Williams' Tavern and got drunk.

7 July. Sun.
    Sold in Mansfield to Mrs. Lambright, ½ lb.
    cheese..   .05.
    Sold to Billy Stump, the use of 3 balls & my
    M 1803, exclusive of powder, to shoot at the
    mark in Central Park ....   .10.

He won 2nd prize—cotton suspenders—which he tried to
sell me for 35 ¢. He got his price later from Mrs. Cooper,
who bought them for her son, Henry. Sarah said,
    "My brother's to home, sickened of the pukes. Fanny,
too."

9 July. 6 AM.
    Anxious for Fanny. Awake all night.

    Bought of Barr & Keys, Chillicothe, 1 copper
    Worm, 6 convolutions, 2½ ft. long .... $3.00.
    Paid in full to Daniel Russel, the charges of
    carrying the above to Mansfield ....   .65.
    Bought of John Lambright, 30 bushels, Indian
    corn, to make whisky. @ 40 ¢............................   12.00.

Hattie Lambright, smoking a cigar: "T'aint the cholera.
They ain't got the shits. Nothing to fret about. Henry and
Fanny will be all right."

10 July.
    Bought of John Chapman, 2 apple trees, 3 yrs.
    old @ 2½ cents, to be paid this fall on demand,
    for which I sold him ½ lb. cheese, amounting to
    the same sum..   .05.
                                                 .05.

Chapman is famous in these parts for his eccentric appear-
ance: shaggy black beard, bare feet, pasteboard visor, and
ragged pantaloons. Sometimes he wears a tin saucepan on
his head, which serves as hat and mushpot. He thinks of

himself as a messenger sent into the wilderness, like John the Baptist, to prepare the way for the Revelations of Emanuel Swedenborg. I won't read any of the latter's tracts that Chapman has pressed on me and everyone else around here. He says, "All creation is a sign of God's love." Hence, his passion for apple trees, dirt, and redskins.

He brought with him this afternoon Tommy Lyons, a drunken Delaware buck from Greentown, who stinks of the rancid bear grease he uses to dress his hair. A wolf paw print is tattooed on his left breast. Soon after they arrived, a horned owl shrieked in the hemlock near the creek. Lyons fled.

Chapman: "He fears the owl might be his squaw's spirit. Her name was Embaugh Ex-whey (Water Woman). She died in childbirth with their son last winter. Now she haunts him. That's why he drinks."

11 July.
   Shelled corn all day.

12 July.
   Bought of Martha Seymour, 1 lb. maple sugar,
   for which I sold her 1 lb. cheese, amounting to
   the same sum ....   .10.
                                                                        .10.
   Bought of Phil Seymour, 1 oaken keg, with
   heads, of 5 gallons ....   .40.

Phil gave me 3 qts. of especially yeasty barm from his Still for a ferment. Their father asked about Tommy Lyons visiting my place yesterday. "If he shows his face around here, I'll kill him."

He wants to kill all the Indians at Greentown, even the children. "Nits breed lice."

13 July.
Paid in full to Mother Beam on the Rocky
Fork, for cracking 300 lbs. my shelled corn to
make mash... .28.

Her husband, Jacob, being sick of a summer fever &
catarrh, she loaded Willy with me, then said, henceforth
their price for the above will be 30 ¢.
I agreed without haggling. There was already the risk of
getting caught in the dark riding home.

14 July. Sun. 8 AM.
Practiced reloading in the saddle at a trot. Phil Seymour
drops his bullet, without being patched, from his mouth into
a charged breech, rams it home, then fires. But without
priming the pan. How?

16 July.
John Chapman owes me to pay this fall on
demand 1 apple tree, 4 yrs. old, at 2½ ¢, for
which I sold him ¼ lb. cheese, amounting to the
same sum... .025.
.025.

He was here to spread the word: Fanny will be a widow
by midnight. Her husband, Henry, was bit on the right foot
by a rattlesnake this afternoon—he'll be the first white man
to die in Richland County. He's bid us take leave of him; a
two mile ride alone thro' the bush for me.
Chapman, on Liz, has already informed the Seymours and
Beams. He will continue S. along the Black Fork about ½
mile to the Lambrights, thence another 1½ miles to the
Lewises and Coffinberrys.

7 PM.
Sold here to the Lambrights, 1 pint cream......... .16.

Their gift for the Coopers. I'll give 1½ lb. cheese left from my last batch. Lambright also brought along a quart of rum. His wife downed a dram. Scared of Indians, she insists we journey together.

17 July.

Young Cooper, dead since 8:20 PM, was laid out in his ruffled shirt, gingham trowsers, no shoes. His right foot and ankle were black and swelled; the skin was split between the first two toes.

On the mantel, with divers other gifts, ½ lb. green hyson tea @ $1.50—from Beam, who got his money's worth consoling Fanny. She said,

"Henry wanted a bite of lunch, but I insisted, 'First fetch my firewood,' and sent him to his death. Because he couldn't see over the armful of logs coming back, he stepped on the snake in his path. I must always have my way."

She brushed a fly off the blackened foot.

10 yr. old Sarah called, "Hear that, Pa? Henry's alive. His backside went off."

Strolled outside, within earshot of Chapman arguing with the Seymours. The latter two had dug Henry's grave under a hollow Red Cedar (*Juniperus virginiana*, Linnaeus), hoping to end 4 yrs. of friendship between the Rev. Cooper and Chief Armstrong.

C. returned with me to the cabin. As I understand him, the Indians will take the proximity of grave & sacred tree "for the grossest impiety" and will not attend Henry's funeral.

I slept three hours in the barn between Beam and Lambright, who snores. Sure enough, no sign of Chief Armstrong and his Delaware.

Immediately after sunup, a Methodist funeral. The Rev. met the coffin as it was carried out the cabin door and walked before it, reading John XI 25–26, Job XIX 25–27 &

1 Tim. VI. After it was laid in the earth, he read again, from Job XIV 1–2 & "The Sunday Service of the Methodists in North America., With Other Occasional Services" (London, 1784, p. 131.). Viz.,

"Thou knowest, Lord, the secrets of our hearts. Shut not thy merciful ears to our prayer." Etc.

Then the Rev. said, "My son, Henry, had beautiful hands and was vain of them. When he got tired, his left eyelid drooped. He worried about his thinning hair. He could whistle and hum at the same time. He was a good man with a plow and an axe. Also a crack shot. But for the life of him, he couldn't spell or do sums. His hero was Gen. Washington, and his favorite verse,

> Better lore did never Science,
> Teach to man than self-reliance.
> Tis the law of Him Who made you—
> Aid yourself and God will aid you.

"He wooed and wed the prettiest girl in Harrisburg, Pennsylvania, and was going to be a father. He was 23 years old. Now he's dead. In the words of Scripture, 2 Samuel 18: 33. 'O, my son, Absalom! My son, my son, Absalom! Would God I had died for thee, O Absalom, my son, my son!' "

Fanny pregnant!

Beam, still with a bad chest cold, tells me that toward the end he slipped young Cooper his canteen filled with French Brandy. "By the time his Ma got a whiff of his breath, the kid was tight as a ring-bolt. Asked her blessing and croaked."

When my vestryman, Avery Arnold, lay dying of a rattlesnake's bite, in Blue Hill, back in Maine, I read him Psalms. He said that the verse, "Whither shall I go from Thy spirit and whither shall I flee thy presence?" gave him creeps.

Peering down at his bloody stool in the chamber pot beside the bed, he asked, "Can Faith make a clean thing from that?"

Weeping, he passed another stool over his bedclothes. Then he said, "Everything looks yellow." And wept on & off another hour or so before dying at 3 PM.

That night, on his kitchen table, I wrote "The Tree of Life."

> I hung from three nails
> On the wind-swept tree
> Six hours
> For My Father's love of thee.
> Love Me.

19 July.

Here late this morn., riding home with his wife, Lambright wore young Cooper's shoes; Fanny's gift to replace his leaky cowhide boots. The Lambrights look alike—plump, fair-haired. Both smoke cigars.

Said Mrs. Lambright, "I understand you're a widower, Brother Keene."

"For eight years."

"You must have married young."

"That's very kind of you," says I.

"Not at all," says she. "I imagine you and Johnny Chapman are about the same age."

"I never thought about it."

"Then do so," she said. "Fanny won't be a widow long."

"Pregnant? I'm not so sure."

"Ever had kids, Tom?"

"No."

"We lost all four."

"Another man's kid is better than no kid at all," Lambright said. "You, Phil Seymour, and Chapman; Fanny ain't got much of a choice."

Me, Chapman & Phil, our junior by 10 yrs., who has a thick, black head of hair, all his teeth, and $.

Apart from Beam and old man Seymour, Chapman is our largest landowner, having within the last month bought another Quarter Section on the flats of the Rocky Fork's west bank. He pays $19.20 per yr. toward a total of $400. for his 160 acres. He's already transplanted 50 apple cuttings there from a nursery he's owned since 1807 on the N. bank of Owl Creek in Knox County.

20 July.
Sold to Bob Coffinberry at his forge on
Diamond St., Mans., 3 lbs. of cheese, for which
he enlarged the touch hole of my rifle,
amounting to the same sum ....   .30.
                                                          .30.

Enabling me to reload at a fast trot by priming the closed pan with a trickle of powder directly from the breech. However, as the barrel's rifling can't engage the unpatched ball, its flight is erratic; I missed a fence post at 20 yds. The shot brought Levi Jones out of his store with his brass blunderbuss cocked & a spiked tomahawk in his belt. He confessed expecting an Indian attack because of the Seymours' insult to Chief Armstrong.

"Very grave," said he, laughing at his own pun.

Bob Coffinberry was not amused; they're in business together, trading with the Delaware: French flints & English gunpowder, bars of lead, knives, belt axes, tomahawks, etc., for beaver skins, a 10 weight of which, depending on quality, brings from $30. to $65. in Canton.

Coffinberry said, "Not one of them bucks has been to town since the funeral."

Jones: "Wait till they run out of powder."

"That could be another month, you goddamned fool. You know how much that'll cost us?"

21 July. Sun. night.

Rain all day washed away some of that Delaware cross-bred corn behind the barn; I replaced the rotted clapboard above Juno's stall & caught cold. Neither a pt. of booze, nor a qt. steaming catnip tea prevented my fever rising about 4 PM.

22 July.
Cloudy till 1 PM.

Phil Seymour made it clear he won't compete for Fanny. Near sundown, after checking my Still, he wished me luck with tomorrow's run. He said,

"Good luck with Fanny, too. I got my hands full looking after my sister Martha till that damned fool Wallace gets back from Harrisburg and marries her."

Which leaves the field to myself & Chapman, about whom Phil told yet another story:

"Summer before last, I come out of Slocum's Tavern in Mount Vernon, and lo and behold, cross the street Johnny's preaching Swedenborg's Heavenly Doctrine on a stump. Half of Knox County is laughing at him. An old man wearing a speckled waistcoat asks, 'You say it rains in Heaven?'

" 'It does,' Chapman says.

" 'And a man must make his living the same way as here?'

"Chapman says, 'He works at the same job. Yes.'

"The old man says, 'Do people die in Heaven?'

"Says Chapman, 'They do not.'

" 'Well,' says the old man. 'That fixes me.'

"Chapman asks, 'How so?'

"And the old man says, 'I'm a grave digger.' "

24 July.
Provided gratis by me at last night's party (men only) on the occasion of my Still's 1st run, 12 gall. whisky, of 80 proof, @ .32 per gall.

Old man Seymour shot out a candle at 30 yards. Phil won the tomahawk throw. Chapman wore those cotton suspenders that Stump sold Mrs. Cooper. A gift from Fanny, says C. Does she fancy him? My cold is back.

25 July.
   Paid to Jacob Beam at his mill on this beginning
   of Dog Days, for cracking 350 lbs. of my corn
   to make mash .... .35.

Compared symptoms of pneumonia. We recovered a week apart, toward the end of Nov., 3 yrs. ago.

About noon, Tommy Lyons appeared, armed with scalping knife, tomahawk and musket. Greasy black paint smeared over his face.

I asked Beam, "Why the black paint?"

"He's in mourning."

They shook each other's left hand, Indian fashion. Lyons' message from Chief Armstrong, via Beam, was for the Rev.:

1. The Chief has enjoined his warriors, women, slaves, to mourn young Cooper's death 12 days, abstaining during that time from all entertainments, etc.—a great honor for an American (Me-hun-she-ke-khan).

2. The Chief craves the pleasure of speaking with his brother at the next full moon, but in his lodge, not the Rev.'s farm.

Meaning, says Beam, that Chapman is right: Armstrong is deeply offended. No Delaware will ever again set foot any where near young Cooper's grave. Henceforth, the Rev. must palaver with Armstrong in Greentown; a round trip, partly thro' wetlands, of almost 5 miles.

Said Beam, "The Seymours are getting a little of their own back after eight years."

"For what?"

"Mrs. Seymour was drownded by a band of drunken bucks in Paint Creek outside Chillicothe, near the Ayres' place.

Ayre's boy, who was fishing, seen everything from behind a cottonwood. Them bucks—three Delaware and a Shawanoe—grabbed her bonnet, cut loose her mare, then tipped her wagon over the bank into the water. Phil found her body the next morning caught on a snag about a mile downstream."

"What happened to the Indians?"

"They got clean away. Phil was so sick he spent all fall and the best part of the winter abed."

I turned down Beam's offer to deliver the message with him, scared of giving Fanny my cold. Fever again, on & off since sunset; chills, between.

11 PM.   My 2nd dose, within the hour, of hemlock bark tea, which Beam swears cured his cough.

26 July.   Fri.

At dawn today, Mrs. Lambright, who brought me ½ doz. roasted apples, said,

"Fanny asked after you last night. Been feeling poorly, as well. No fear. All she wants is three of these for breakfast every morning. A purging won't do you no harm, neither."

Nor good.

27 July.   11:30 AM.

Fanny arrived with the Rev., and a Bannock cake, to which she adds stewed pumpkin. She has put on weight since the funeral.

I mentioned Lambright's gratitude for young Cooper's shoes. She said,

"They gave me hope of him. Henry had those shoes made from Spanish leather in Chillicothe for our wedding. Every body grinned because they squeaked. Who knows? Our Savior at the Latter Day might have done the same. Johnny Chapman tells me not to fret about Henry being buried in his bare feet. He preaches that the New Jerusalem is come; there won't be no Latter Day."

Seated sideways at my table, his long legs crossed, the Rev.
said,

"These are pretty pots for your ink and pounce, Brother
Keene. Where from? England?"

"Staffordshire."

"Very pretty indeed," he said, running his finger over a
gilded rim. "Brother Jones tells me you've begun a Waste
Book. I can't approve profits from a Still, but admire your
keeping account of them. Am I a hypocrite?"

"No," said I. "A Yankee, like myself."

He said, "I keep a Diary in cipher; a short hand of my
own devising. You think that queer?"

"Not for a Yankee. A Parson I once knew in Cambridge
did the same."

"Did he say why?"

"He believed writing down his sins in Plain English was
tantamount to repeating them."

"And so it is. What was your Parson's name?"

"Richard Pendleton. Actually, he was my tutor in Hebrew
at the College."

"I took you months ago for an educated man," said he.
"Ask Henry."

Fanny whispered, "He forgets," into my left ear.

Before they left, the Rev. asked me, "One favor, please."

"If I'm able."

"Say something in the Lord's tongue."

"Amen."

Fanny's glance made me apologize, then recite,

$$\text{יְבָרֶכְךָ יְהֹוָה וְיִשְׁמְרֶךָ:}$$
$$\text{יָאֵר יְהֹוָה פָּנָיו אֵלֶיךָ וִיחֻנֶּךָ:}$$
$$\text{יִשָּׂא יְהֹוָה פָּנָיו אֵלֶיךָ וְיָשֵׂם לְךָ שָׁלוֹם:}$$

The Lord bless thee, and keep thee;
The Lord make His face shine upon thee, and be
   gracious unto thee;

The Lord lift up His countenance upon thee, and
> give thee peace. (Num. 6:24–26).

Could I bring myself to kiss the inflamed black jaw's bite
on Fanny's chin? It nauseates me.

Her blue eyes are small & widely set in her broad face
with its high cheekbones.

I have touched her but once—shaking hands, when we
first met in Central Park, Mans., on Sunday, April 7, 1811.

She wore her hair up today, leaving two curls at the nape
of her neck.

A characteristic gesture when she speaks: tapping those
thin fingers of her right hand on her chest, which is freshly
sunburnt. The tip of her nose is peeling.

Last month I overheard a nasty argument about money
between her and Henry—he was stingy. Fanny gave as good
as she got. I like her spunk.

4 AM.
> Sunt quas eunuchi imbelles, ac mollia semper
> Oscula delectent, et desperatio barbae,
> Et quod abortivo non est opus. Illa voluptas
> Summa tamen, quod jam calida matura juventa
> Inguina traduntar medicis, jam pectine nigro.
> Ergo expectatos ac jussos crescere primum
> Testiculos, postquam coeperunt esse bilibres,
> Tonsoris tantum damno rapit Heliodorus. . . .
> Conspicuus longe cunctisque notabilis intrat
> Balnea, nec dubie custodem vitis et horti
> Provocat a domina, factus spado. Dormiat ille
> Cum domina. . . .

28 July. Sun. 6 AM.
For the first time in 15 yrs., the Juvenal verse has no
power to arouse me. A piss hard-on only, gone upon relieving
myself at sunup—4:55.

Some girls love eunuchs.
Smooth cheeks & no worry about abortions.
But their delight is in a boy
But their delight is in a boy
Whose chest & private parts are overgrown with
Black hair before being
given to the surgeons

Some girls love eun

Some girls like eunuchs
With smooth cheeks.
No worry about abortions.
But they love a boy
Whose privates are covered
With black hair;
Whose testicles are allowed
To ripen before the surgeon Heliodorus
Cuts them off.
The observed of all observers,
A challenge to the god of gardens and vineyards,
He enters the baths,
Castrated at his lady's command.
Now he may sleep with his Mistress. . . .

Even translating the Juvenal didn't arouse me.

7:30 AM. Juno & Willy are frantic with pain. 4 months here, and I can't get used to the necessity of grazing stock by night, when the black jaws in the bush are quiescent. They look like small flies. The genus, perhaps species, probably not yet classified. *Stimulus amoris* (Keene)?

9 PM. Looser phlegm, as Beam promised, but last night's want of sleep coupled with the early morn.'s miasma has aggravated my intermittent fever, chills, which kept me from going to town.

The Lambrights brought me a squirrel pie for supper & the news. Neither Fanny, Sarah, nor Mrs. Cooper attended

Methodist Meeting; today marks 4 months since Martha Seymour has received a letter from her betrothed; Billy Stump's wife writes from her brother's house in Cincinnati that she & their 2 kids count the hours till he earns the $40 for their journey here. Phil Seymour's 3 shots at the 75 yd. offhand match won him a First Prize worth $12—a 6 × 4 blue Damask silk shawl, which he gave to his sister.

Lambright copied the following, verbatim, from Thursday's "The Chillicothe Independent Republican":

> Riflemen Attention! A man will be shot for the benefit of his wife and children—$1 a shot—one hundred yards distance, with rifles—on Sunday, the 27th instant., in front of Slocum's Tavern, Mount Vernon Township, Knox County, at 3 PM.
>
> The fore-mentioned man is in a very low state of health and wishes to leave his family snug.

29 July.

My left lung remains congested, the hemlock bark tea has no effect.

A run of 14 gall. whisky of 80 proof from my Still.

30 July.

Paid to Jacob Beam at his mill, for cracking 350 lbs. my corn to make mash, for which I sold him 1 gall., 3 gills whisky of 80 proof .... .35.

.35.

Beam suggested,

"Go back home, cut as many notches in a stick as you get chills over the next twelve hours, then throw it over your left shoulder into the creek without looking back. Your chills will go away with it."

31 July.

Given gratis this morn. at his mill to Jacob Beam, 1 gall. whisky, of 80 proof, at 32 ¢.

Beam learned the cure from Montour, the old Delaware medicine man—Tommy Lyons's father.

"They don't get along," said Beam. "Tommy Lyons drinks too much."

"What's the old man got against booze?"

"He don't like flints and steel, neither; nor woolen stuffs nor ploughs. Not even guns. Nothing from whites. Like Tecumseh. He's Tecumseh's man in Greentown, if you ask me."

3 PM.

Sold to John Chapman, ¼ lb. cheese................ .025.
He owes me to pay this fall on demand, 9 (nine)
more apple trees, not less than 3 years old, @
.025, for which I'm sworn to read "Heaven &
Its Wonders & Hell From Things Heard &
Seen," by Emanuel Swedenborg, Translated by
V. Crudge from the Latin, "De Coelo et Ejus,
etc." "The New Church of Promoting the
Heavenly Doctrines of the New Jerusalem by
translating & publishing The Theological Writ
of the Hon. Em. Swedenborg, Great East
Cheap, Eng. 1801." amounting to the same sum   .225.
  .225.

"Here's Fresh News from Heaven," said C., handing me the book. "It's been a great consolation to Fanny."

10:20 PM.
Given gratis to myself, 1 pint whisky.

1 August.
I have in ready money .... $1.105.

Half-way thro' Swedenborg's book. He is a mystic. Believes we don't die, but become angels, retaining our human form; every sense, memory, thought, & affection intact.

2 August.
Bought of Levi Jones, at his store, Mans., 6
sheets Royal size drawing paper, @ .03, for
which I sold him ½ gall. whisky, of 80 proof,
amounting to the same sum .... .18.
.18.

Bought of the above, 4 sticks, India ink, @ .11;
and 4 oz. white lead at .025, for which I sold
him 1½ gall. whisky, of 80 proof, amounting to
the same sum.. .46.
.46.

3 August. 7:15 PM.
Even with spectacles, I can no longer draw by candlelight.
My last illustration, also of a text, was done with the naked
eye, before the fire in my study at Blue Hill. "And be not
drunk with wine, wherein is excess; but be filled with the
Spirit." Eph. 5:18. woodcut, Jan. 1804.

4 August. 8 AM.
Am in excess, 1 pt. whisky, 80 proof.
8 PM.
Another run of 14 gall. whisky, 80 proof.

5 August.
My reward for giving Mrs. Cooper a shoulder from a fat
buck I shot at dawn by the hemlock: a supper of corn mush,
served without salt, which she saves for dining on the
Sabbath.
Her conversation was about her husband, who meets with
Armstrong tomorrow night. The Rev. is out ministering to
his flock S. along the Black Fork nearest Greentown, viz.,
the Lewis family, and Bob Coffinberry's younger brother
Geo., his wife, 3 kids, who settled there this spring.
She ignores Fanny. Their affections are more strained
since young Cooper's death.
Sarah asked, "What's round on each end but high in the
middle?"

Fanny said, "I give up."

"Brother Keene?"

"You got me."

"Ohio. Get it now? O-high-o."

Sarah then said, "I thought that riddle up myself."

"You mustn't lie," Fanny told her. "Johnny Chapman told you that riddle."

The Cooper family lives according to the Methodist Discipline. They arise at 4 AM, meditate on Scripture, pray; ditto for another hour at 5 PM. The Rev. fasts every Fri.; while the others sup, he reads aloud a chapter from "The Causes, Evils, & Cures of Church & Heart Divisions" (New York City, 1807).

Fanny's family were among the first Methodists in Harrisburg. She would never marry again without the Rev.'s consent, i.e., his wife's.

6 August.

Awakened last night by the horned owl's shriek.

Sunset. Cannot incorporate the following text into the design of my paintings:

I talked with three who were dead three days, mentioning that their bodies were buried. They were smitten with surprise, saying, "We are alive."

(Em. Swedenborg, "Heaven etc. & Hell etc." Chap. XLVI, 'The Resuscitation of Man from the Dead & his entrance, External Life.' 452.)

7 August.

Sold to John Lambright, ½ pt. whisky of 80 proof .... .040.

Sold to the above, ¼ lb. cheese .... .025.

Courtesy of the Thomas Keene Collection, Mansfield, Ohio.

8 August.
   Paid to Jacob Beam at his mill, for cracking 300
   lbs. my corn to make mash, for which I sold
   him 1 gall. less 2 gills whisky of 80 proof.......... .30.
                                                        .30.
   9 PM.
   My left lung has been free of any congestion a full 24 hrs.

9 August. 8:30 PM.
   Chapman just left with his book. I showed him my painting.
He awaits a message from Henry, via his own Guardian
Spirit. "She whispers in my left ear. Spirits spoke with
Swedenborg by looking into his eyes—the way thoughts are
shared in Heaven."

10 August.
   Bought of Phil Seymour, 1 pouch big enough
   for 8 flints, for which I sold him 1½ gall.
   whisky, of 80 proof, amounting to the same
   sum .... .50.
                                                        .50.

   A fair exchange; he dresses the inside of a weasel's pelt,
then, with needle & thread, narrows & shortens the aperture.
One flint at a time pops from its mouth.
   Phil tells me he's hired Billy Stump for $3.00 plus victuals
& use of an ox to grub out the 3 girdled black walnut trees
near the old Indian burial ground. In this heat, counting
Sundays, the job will take Stump 2½ weeks.
   Said I, "That's a dollar a week less than I was paid for
mowing hay in Pennsylvania."
   "You should taste Martha's roasted pigeon stuffed with
mushrooms. Or her blueberry pudding. Believe me, Stump
got hisself a good deal. He says his wife ain't worth shit as a
cook."

11 August. Sun. night.
Sold to Williams at his Tavern, Mans., 9 lbs.
cheese.. .90.
Sold to the above, 5 gall. whisky, of 80 proof .... $1.60.

The same price for booze charged him by old man Seymour now that the Delaware have resumed trading peltry under the beeches in Central Park.

10 PM. *Masturbatus sum.* Thoughts of the young bare-breasted Delaware squaw I saw this morn. at the corner Park Ave. E. & Diamond St. She paints her nipples, cheeks & eyelids bright red, yet has the air of modesty common to all Del. women. The Rev. can not make Armstrong understand this is provocative to white men.

12 August.
Another run of 12 gall. whisky, 80 proof. Before clouding up about 2 PM, the sky turned green.

13 August.
In the east, at the height of last night's storm, a crash of trees sounded like one continuing peal of thunder. Next spring, violets, blue phlox, & wild hyacinth will grow in the sunlight midst the uprooted rotten trunks.

14 August.
The Rev.'s eyelids are swelled & red from 5 days & nights of powwowing in Armstrong's smoky lodge. Useless. The Chief now refuses to free his female negro slave—a Methodist named Lettiece Shipman—till after the harvest, which must be gathered by squaws in honor of Ka-ha-suna, Our Mother, the Earth.

Mrs. Cooper blames old man Seymour. "May God forgive him. I can not."

"As he cannot forgive those Indians who murdered his wife," the Rev. said.

"Are they then the ones to blame?" Fanny asked. "What about the white man whose liquor made them drunk? Is he the cause? No, Johnny is right. We know only of effect in this life; the cause is hid above. Like Johnny says, Henry's death wasn't my fault."

Mrs. Cooper said, "I forbid you mention that heathen in my house."

Chapman has told her that the famous story of his remorse upon killing a rattlesnake is true. It happened the Sept. before last while he was mowing grass on the Bullock farm near Perrysville.

She quoted him saying,

" 'The poor critter started me and I squashed its skull with the heel of my scythe. In my ungodly passion, I squashed its skull with one blow.' "

"He told me that less than twenty-four hours after Henry's death. The morning you buried your husband, woman."

Fanny said, "The snake ain't to blame, neither. The cause is hid above."

16 August. Noon.

Borrowed Jones' brass blunderbuss, which I loaded with 2 oz. gravel, and, with one shot, killed 15–20 of the blackbirds in my corn. Now, immediately upon my raising the barrel, the birds call out to each other & scatter. I will lose 23–30 bushels to them.

My horned owl spent an hour this morn. perched on her hemlock, staring directly into the sun.

A riddle for Sarah: Jones, who speaks some Del., asks why the Indians call us whites horned owls (Ko ko-suk). The answer: Because these owls hatch their eggs only in nests stolen from red-tailed hawks, who must also surrender their hunting grounds to them.

11 PM. I drink myself to sleep every night lest thoughts of the naked eunuch commanded by his Mistress to fondle her breasts make me abuse myself. Abby couldn't banish the Juvenal verse from my mind because she was frigid in her

affection. Also scrawny. Trying to imagine Fanny naked and abed.

18 August.   Sun.
    Sold to Williams, at his Tavern, Mans., 5 gall.
    whisky, 80 proof.. $1.60.
    Sold to the above, 4 lbs. cheese.......................... .40.
    Sold to Billy Stump, the use of 3 balls, my M
    1803, exclusive of powder, to shoot at the mark
    in Central Park.. .10.

He finally won First Prize—5 pecks of salt worth $2.00, which Jones donated. Stump sold it for $2.50 to Phil. He & Tommy Lyons threw their tomahawks from 10 paces at a piece of foolscap, 3″ square, nailed to a beech. At dusk, they declared the match a draw, went off to Williams' and got drunk. Chapman, at the bar, said to me,

"Tommy Lyons was really shook by that owl at your place the other day. He's sure it was his squaw. He got no defense against evil spirits. He's ah-lux-soo, poor soul. Empty. He's never had a Vision; no guardian angel protects him. That ain't usual for a Delaware Indian. He's specially shamed cause his Pa's a great Ma-ta-en-noo (medicine man)."

19 August.   10:15 PM.
    In whisky veritas. When Abby died, I was left alone with the Juvenal. Fearing I had been delivered into Satan's hands, I denied my faith rather than face God's wrath. I left Blue Hill and became a common laborer, and worked my way south to Pennsylvania.
    Within a year, I learned I could live without God. Why now such terror of death?

20 August.
    Given gratis at the eve.'s celebration, Beam's
    Mill, 3 gall. whisky, 80 proof, at 96 ¢.

Old man Seymour grudgingly contributed the same. Just back from 3 days with his banker in Chillicothe, he says Anthony Wayne's victory 17 yrs. ago today at Fallen Timbers no longer means a damn; save the Del., those Indian Nations which afterward made peace at Greene Ville are at this moment rallying to Tecumseh & his brother encamped some 30 odd miles NE of Vincennes, Ind.

Up against several thousand warriors armed by the British, Harrison's Indiana & Kentucky militiamen must wait on the arrival from Pittsburgh of the 4th Reg. U.S. Infantry: the only trained riflemen Eastern politicians in Washington City will spare in our defense.

The time to celebrate, says old man Seymour, will be when Harrison burns the redskins out & takes the scalps of the 2 Shawanoe brothers.

"Make no mistake," said he. "Tecumseh plans to butcher us all. Every white in the Northwest Territory. He boasts about it. His brother hands out magic beans that will turn our bullets into big drops of water. Don't laugh. The bucks gathering round his lodge-pole believe anything he says. And he says their chiefs had no right to sell the Federal Government any land. The land, he says, don't belong just to the Miami or Delaware; even the Shawanoe don't own their hunting grounds."

Beam: "Say what?"

"You heard. He says the Shawanoe will share with their brothers to hunt between the Ohio and Lake Erie. Him and Tecumseh know that making one Nation of all Indians is their last hope of driving us out."

Sam Lewis: "Not the Delaware. I hope." His new cabin is a short walk from Greentown.

The Rev. said, "The Delaware abide by the Greene Ville Treaty; likewise the Miami and Potawatomi. Their chiefs met with Harrison again at Fort Wayne two years back. As friends. Armstrong's son, Silas, was there. Sober, too. He brung his Pa back maybe $900 worth of salt, calico, scissors and thread. Also two Lehigh Valley rifles, flints, powder and shot."

Chapman called out,

"Understand this. 17 years ago today, Chief Armstrong and Montour fought alongside Tecumseh's Shawanoe scouts when they ambushed Wayne's left flank on the Maumee. A great honor for two Delaware warriors, believe me.

"The point being, Armstrong accepted those goods as his due. You can't bribe a Delaware warrior. We're talking here of Pom-chip-hic-a (Sits Down Spotted). He is a Leni Lenape war chief, of the Turtle Band, who's sworn himself and his people to peace."

Phil said, "He must be sixty-five. What happens when he dies?"

24 August.
Sold to the Rev. Ezra Cooper, ½ lb. cheese........   .05.

He asked, "Did Newton hold to Scripture on Creation?"

"He did."

"How would he have accounted for this patch of Indian corn?"

"I don't follow you."

"This here yellow dent is a cross between hard flint and flower bred by redskins," said he. "I've done so myself."

"What of it?"

"Being man made, it couldn't have been here on the evening of the Sixth Day of Creation. What do you make of that?"

"It's a mystery to me. Also to Linnaeus."

"Who's Linnaeus?"

I explained. He said, "We're kin to bats?"

"According to his system of classification, yes. Just as the sweetbriar is related to the rose."

"But he held all things to have been created by God in six days?"

"Yes."

"And this man Swedenborg?"

"He too."

Said he, "Fanny likes his book. But he can't explain how yellow dent corn comes to be, can he?"

"Nobody can."

"That's painful to me. I lack faith."

9 PM. Yellow dent corn could have originated from pollen scattered by wind. More to the Rev.'s point: Coffinberry's deliberate crossing of his white gourdseed from Va. with the above, which produces a new breed, sweeter than all.

25 August. Sun.
Sold to Williams at his Tavern, Mans., 3 gall.
whisky, 80 proof... .96.

No shoot today in Central Park; we decided to conserve powder and shot, after reading in "The Chillicothe Independent Republican" that on July 31, a large meeting at Vincennes, resolved

"That the safety of the persons & property of this frontier can be secured only by the breaking up of the combination formed by Tecumseh, the Shawanoe war chief, on the Wabash,"

All commissioned & staff officers of the 2nd Brigade, 2nd Div., Ohio Militia, have been notified to muster at Portsmouth, on the 9 Sept., 1811, by Matthew Clark Nelson, Major Gen., 2nd Div., Ohio Militia.

Old man Seymour, who (naturally) knows Nelson, says the Division is at half strength, woefully armed. It was promised 200 new M 1803's, of which less than 30 ever reached Chillicothe.

I told of buying my weapon for $15 in October 1809 from a blacksmith in Canton. Chapman said,

"You're an accomplice with a thief. That rifle was stolen; it's the property of the Federal Government."

26 August.

    Paid to Jacob Beam at his mill for cracking 350
lbs. my corn, for which I sold him 1 gall., 3 gills
whisky of 80 proof..   .35.

    .35.

28 August.

    Mrs. Lambright asked, "Do you hanker after Fanny?"

"Yes."

    "Then get your arse over there, for Christ's sake. Talk
with her. Marry the girl!"

    Lambright's impressed by my M 1803, particularly the
large caliber. His Lancaster County rifle takes a much smaller
ball—55 per lb. He advises I buy a tomahawk like his.

    "When you fight in the bush, you want to be able to axe
a body, as well as shoot him. Ever fit a battle, Brother
Keene?"

    "Never."

    "You might yet," he said. "Get yourself a hawk."

29 August.

    This morn., Fanny said, "Of course, Johnny suffered from
killing that snake. Any living thing. He won't light a fire in
the bush for fear of harming bugs."

    I wanted to ask, "Is Johnny my rival for your affections?"
but didn't have the courage.

    She's begun to show.

31 August.

    Another run of 14 gall. whisky, 80 proof.

1 Sept.   Sun.

I have in ready money .... $6.78.

Bought of Levi Jones, Mans., 1¼ lb. American
rifle powder, finely ground, for which I sold
him 4 gall. whisky, 80 proof, amounting to the
same sum .... $1.25.

1.25.

No news from Indiana in "The Chill. Ind. Rep." An article
from Philadelphia predicts that the new Congress sitting next
month will declare War upon Great Britain over the objections
of the Federalists & their New England supporters, who
undoubtedly include my former flock at Blue Hill.

How will I behave under fire? Lambright says a musket
ball hisses when it hits wood near your head. "Never duck.
Don't move a muscle. Above all, don't jerk the trigger and
waste your shot."

5 Sept.

Masturbatus sum this morn., after turning out the turnips.
Imagined the eunuch commanded to bathe his Mistress with
a sponge in a marble pool, then fuck her. Hence, my
procrastination about asking the Rev.'s permission to court
Fanny.

10:30 PM.   Drunk.

6 Sept.

Bought from Levi Jones, at his store, Mans.,
one tomahawk-hatchet. 2 lb. head—iron with a
steel cutting edge—fitted on an 18-inch long
hickory haft .... .67.

7 Sept.

Chopped and stacked 4 cords of wood—my winter's supply.
Also practiced what I learned yesterday from Phil about
throwing my tomahawk (Del.: Tom-mo-heek-con).

You let the axe loose overhead at the top of an easy swing. Its weight does the rest. Like squeezing off a shot, Phil says, it must seem to happen by itself.

I concentrate on letting the haft slip thro' my right hand the instant my left foot hits the ground. The axe flies in the air. At its apex, it flips over once, then falls head-first into the target: a knothole in an oak 10 paces off. Or should.

Phil fears his sister & Billy Stump have taken a shine to one another. Old man Seymour has kept the latter on as a hired hand to strip & grade 1200 odd lbs. of tobacco, worth over $130 in Mt. Vernon.

Phil says, "Money is what Pa cares for. Martha's good name don't mean nothing to him. Well, it does to me. She's all I got."

9 Sept.

Wild turkeys in my corn. Have this day alone clubbed to death & burned 64. Lambright thinks we may be forced to harvest before the corn is ripe.

He & Hattie were in Mans. yesterday, where the price per bushel has already doubled to 80 ¢. Still no news from Indiana. Nor a letter for Martha Seymour. Only the Rev.'s latest copy of "The Methodist Messenger," a pamphlet published in New York City, which Hattie borrowed to give me an excuse to return it & see Fanny.

I should have known. The Rev. is also among the poets. His 20 lines of verse, entitled "Oppression," end,

> Sons of pity, let your bosoms,
> Warn'd, with indignation flow.
> Rouse with spirit worthy freemen,
> Save the tortured slaves from woe.

Lambright says that Everett Hunt, the publisher of "The Chill. Ind. Rep.," wouldn't print the above for fear of offending his subscribers (& advertisers) in Ross County, who are originally from Kentucky & Virginia: "Southerners who shoved that damn'd Black Code down our throats."

"What's that?"

He explained. Since 1807, no negro has been allowed to settle in this State unless he can, within 20 days, provide a $500 bond signed by 2 white men who guarantee his good behavior.

I asked about Armstrong's black slave girl. "How will the Rev. come up with that kind of cash?"

"It ain't necessary. This ain't Cincinnati. We don't heed the Black Code in Richland County," Lambright said. "We're all free men here."

12 Sept.

Turkey shit in the fields is ankle-deep. At dawn, when the birds flew down out of their roosts, 4 wolves (*Canis lupus* Linnaeus) rushed them from the bush. They ate two turkeys alive. Flock gone.

Turned out the potatoes—my poor back!

13 Sept.

Received in part from John Chapman, for
reading Swedenborg, 1 apple tree, 3 yrs. old,
which he transplanted near the dead beech on
my hillock.

He begged and received my pardon for calling me an accomplice with a thief.

Am now privy to his chief sin—Love of Self, the one Swedenborg condemns above all others, and why Chapman lost his head over my rifle.

His father was dismissed from the Continental Army in Sept. 1780. An accomplice with a speculator who was arrested on Boston Common for selling 50 lbs. of lard & 2 doz. pickled hams which had been under the former's charge at Salem depot.

C.: "He was a thief. The army let him off easy, because he was a hero of Bunker Hill. A Captain, arisen from the ranks. They didn't want a scandal. He was simply let go. Allowed to keep his sword; a short saber, with a brass pommel in the likeness of a lion's head. But that was all. He got neither a bounty nor land grant for his services.

"He hired out as a farm hand up and down the Connecticut Valley. At home, my step-mother and us kids had to call him 'Captain.' Every one in Longmeadow knew the truth. All the kids at school. We lived two miles below the Springfield line in a frame house. Two rooms for fourteen people. The saber hung over the kitchen mantel. He polished it after Meeting every Sunday.

"I hate him. I love only myself. I'm betrothed to an angel in Heaven."

"That so?"

"Her name is Beth Holland. She's buried behind the Meetinghouse at Longmeadow, Mass., where she first come to me in the afternoon of January 29th, 1790. I was sixteen. She's fourteen. She died of the cancer in her breast, on November 16, 1770, four years before I was born."

14 Sept.
　　Sold to Isaac Williams at his Tavern, Mans., 9
　　lbs. cheese... 　　.90.
　　Sold to the above, 5 gall. whisky, of 80 proof,
　　@ .32 .... 　　$1.60.

For the last three winters, he's allowed Chapman to sleep on his tavern floor, before the fire, for free. "It's good luck to give a lunatick a helping hand."

15 Sept.　Sun.
　　Outside Jones' store in Mans. this Morn., where she bought a bottle of Duffy's Elixir, Fanny said,

"Swedenborg's book gives me word of Henry. By now, two angels have brought him around. They opened his left eye; he sees a dim light. He must spend a year examining his soul. After that, depending on what he finds, he must take himself to Heaven or Hell. Johnny promises to let me know which."

"How?"
"His guardian angel will tell him."

23 Sept.
While spying out Greentown this AM, Phil swapped 2 gall.
of watered whisky for a squaw's fat dog. The stewed flesh
tastes like veal; a welcome change from boiled venison.
Tommy Lyons and Montour aren't speaking. The former
begged his father to drive away his dead squaw's spirit, which
haunts him each dawn in the form of that horned owl. The
old medicine man refused, saying,
"Become a man! Stop drinking whisky! Help yourself!"
Montour has prophesied his own death this coming winter.
He will be replaced by a greater medicine man, identity not
revealed.
Otherwise, says Phil, Greentown is quiet. He saw the
negress—Lettiece Shipman—working with the squaws in the
corn.
Stump, who was sharpening a sickle, asked, "You suppose
the inside of her twat is black?"
Phil: "Shut your filthy mouth."

25 Sept.
Sold here to the Rev. Ezra Cooper, 1 lb. cheese ..... .10.

Returned "The Methodist Messenger" to him.
He said, "I've no illusions about my verse, Brother Keene.
But I know right from wrong. Slavery is a great wrong."
Two years ago, about age 22, Armstrong's negress was set
free in her master's Will. "The gentleman, whose name was
Sloat, doubtless believed himself a Christian. He had learned
her in secret to read from Scripture, and to write. Made her
a Methodist. Then he freed her in his Will, but without a
cent to her name.
"There she was, a black wench on her own in Morehead,
Ky.; all she knowed was 'Go North!' A half-breed trapper
named McFall took her to Cincinnati. They couldn't stay

because of the Black Code. She decided to go to Canada. By this time, McFall wanted to marry her. She said, 'Only in Canada.' They got as far as Slocum's Tavern in Mt. Vernon, where he died of the bloody flux.

"There she was again, flat broke, on her own. She couldn't pay for McFall's coffin. Chief Armstrong was in town. He said, 'Be my slave, and I'll buy you a pine coffin.' Lettiece made the deal. The night of the funeral, she become Armstrong's third wife.

"She—a Methodist!—must dance half-naked at the harvest with the other squaws in honor of a little painted wooden idol called Ka-ha-suna. I promised her I'd set her free."

Have always liked him. He never tries to convert me.

27 Sept.

Paid to Jacob Beam at his mill, for cracking 20 bushels of my corn for which I sold him 2 gills whisky, of 80 proof, amounting to the same sum .... .02.

.02.

Last Sun., at Mans., Montour told him,

"I will die this December. (Na-we-ou-u-ka-so.) You will die December next year."

Beam: "If that red-skinned son of a bitch was aiming to scare me, he did."

28 Sept.

Split wood, hauled mud from the creek to mend my chimney.

29 Sept.

Bought of Jones at his store, Mans., 1 silver thimble, for which I sold him 1 gall. whisky, of 80 proof, amounting to the same sum................ .32.

.32.

30 Sept.

At the Coopers' for Sarah's 11th birthday. Spite her mother-in-law's objections, Fanny gave her a party. Sarah thanked me for the thimble.

Chapman's gift: "Come sit on my lap. This story is about Fanny Fish. Fanny Fish was a girl about your age. She owned two fuffers. Now fuffers are supposed to eat chestnuts. Those two ate her elbows. She took the fuffers to be fixed in the new fuffer factory at Cleveland, off Euclid Road. They then ate grapes."

Sarah asked, "What about her elbows?"

"She didn't shed a drop of blood. Nor feel any pain. In fact, her elbows grew back instantly. That's the thing about fuffers. Behind their fangs on the roof of the mouth, like rattlesnakes, they got two sacks. But filled with fuffer balm. Immediately the fuffer bites, the balm squirts out. Kills all pain, heals the wound, and makes the chewed-off part grow right back. Fuffers hurt, then heal us—like God."

1 Oct.

I have in ready money .... $8.71.

3 Oct.

Sold here to John Chapman, ½ lb. cheese .... .05.

Sold to the above, 2 cups milk .... .04.

Received in part from the above, for reading Swedenborg, 3 apple trees, 3 yrs. old.

Delivered by oxcart.

C. took a crust of bread from the slop bucket outside my door, saying, "Never waste the gifts of a merciful God, Brother Keene." Ate it with his cheese.

He won't touch coffee, tea or tobacco. "I don't want to develop a hankering for them things. They ain't available in Heaven."

Lives mostly on milk & honey. "We read that this is Heavenly food."

8 Oct. 11 PM.

Masturbatus sum. Imagined that young squaw who paints her nipples red. She stands in a trance, facing me at the corner of Park Ave. E. & Diamond St. Naked, save for a necklace of polished elk's teeth. Eyes shut, lips parted, hands by her side, the palms turned out, & fingers spread. Her painted little breasts rise & fall with each breath.

She tries to open her eyes; the lids twitch. Only I can break the spell. That particularly excites me.

9 Oct. 9 PM.

Masturbatus sum. (Juvenal. Eunuch commanded by his Mistress to lick her privates.)

12 Oct. 9 PM.

Drunk.

14 Oct.

Have this day finished picking my first crop here of Indian corn; a yield of 140 bushels from 2 acres. Chapman says, "Ohio is the land of milk and honey."

We both talk Yankee: thro' the nose, with a swing to the words. Likewise young Cooper, who was born in Taunton, Mass. His voice must already be fading from Fanny's memory. She'll soon have trouble recalling his face. Hers warded off the naked eunuch from me these last 2 nights.

15 Oct.

Sold in Mans. to Bob Coffinberry, 1 gall. whisky
of good proof, for which he owes me to select &
deliver 15–20 of his thickest ears of yellow
gourdseed corn for seed.

The above is not only sweeter, but yields ½ more per acre than any previous flinty breed. Yet, as the Rev. observed, no one can explain how such a thing comes to be. That disquiets me, as well.

16 Oct. 3 PM.

Banked my cabin & barn with corn stalks. 15 mins. ago, on the path to the creek, a black she-bear started me. We both cut and run.

She weighs about 300 lbs. Could have provided me with grease enough for the winter; her pelt would have kept me warm. Instead, I must fret till she hibernates; her ravenous appetite is a threat to Juno, my apple trees, the corn.

17 Oct. 4 PM.

The black she-bear again, behind the barn. This time I was armed. I had the patch of white fur on her chest in my sights at less than 50 ft. The wind was right. She neither smelled nor saw me. But I yelled. Held my fire. She peered about with her piggy little eyes, popped her breath between her yellowed fangs, and ambled off.

"I will have mercy on whom I will have mercy." (Rom. 9:15).

18 Oct.

Daubed my cabin.

19 Oct. Sun.

| Sold here to Lambright 1 lb. cheese.................... | .10. |
| "   "   "   1 lb. butter .... | .30. |

Let him my rifle & 6 balls to hunt the bear, whom he glimpsed yesterday digging grubs from a rotten log at the edge of his corn field.

21 Oct.

Finished making 20 lbs. cheese.

Lambright returned my rifle & bullets. For want of a hunting dog, he lost the bear's trail about 2 miles SW of Greentown.

22 Oct.

Today at noon, in her cabin, Fanny said,

"Thank you for loving me, Tom. I'm flattered. Honest. I like you. I've always hankered after older men. Henry was an overgrown boy, under his Ma's thumb.

"I married him because he asked me. All my kin were dead, and there was Henry in Harrisburg, looking over his prospective bride. The Wagner girl, who's the Rev.'s second cousin, once removed. She introduced us. Five days later, we were betrothed. What a to-do. I'm four months gone with his child. A boy, I hope.

"That gives you pause, don't it? Well, imagine my feelings. The baby is fatherless because of me, yet I hate Henry for dying on us. Prayer ain't helped. Only studying Swedenborg's book. It puts my mind at ease to think that Henry might be living in a spiritual world that corresponds exactly to ours. This very minute, he may be sitting snug in the spiritual counterpart of his favorite split-bottom chair; the one by the window. He sets there learning awesome secrets about himself from angels. If he passes muster, he'll go to heaven. He might marry again. A girl who mustn't always have her own way.

"Give me a year, Tom, to sort it out. You know how much I value your opinions on every thing. I want us to talk a lot together.

"Don't be scared, Tom. I won't ask what you think about the baby; leastways, not for a while. By the by, them spectacles become you."

24 Oct.

Last night's frost cracked open the thick outer shells of the nuts scattered under my hickory tree; wrested only half a bushel from the multitude of squirrels. Shot one.

9 PM.

Lines Occasioned By My Shooting at Squirrels.

Two drinks,
And what a shot I am.

After three,
I hit the tree.
A hickory
That goes some 50 feet
Straight up the

The Book of Life.

Two drinks, today
And what a shot I am.
After three,
I hit a hickory
Six feet in breadth:
The requisite depth
For planting flesh.
Flesh must decay.
Not like this book.
This book, which sprouts from rot,
Is here to stay.

26 Oct.

Can't find my compass, which I misplaced while drunk last night.

Discovered this day 3 big patches of ginseng growing in the shade of the beeches near the W. bank of the creek, below the ford. Returned there about 2 PM with my sang hoe & began digging. Tho' some roots have succumbed to fungus, perhaps 90 lbs. remain.

Cleaned & dried, they'll bring me $6.40, which Jones will double by selling them to his agent at Chillicothe. God knows what the root now fetches per lb. in China, given the risks our ships take running the Blockade. Last week's newspaper reports that the Mass. seaman impressed almost 6 months ago off New York City is still being held aboard the British sloop, Belt.

27 Oct. Sun.
Bought of Levi Jones at his store, Mans., 3
pecks of salt, for which I paid him 5 gall.
whisky of 80 proof... $1.60.
                                                   1.60.

Bought of the above, one 1 lb. bar of Dunbar
lead, for which I owe him to pay the 3rd Inst.
Nov. 3½ gall. whisky.

Lambright says I should get drunk again to recall the
whereabouts of my compass. He often hides his patch knife
from himself.

Outside Jones' store, Lambright's wife grabbed my sleeve
& said,

"Next, your hands will tremble all day. You'll hardly be
able to recollect your own name. What will Fanny think?"

"I'm not sure I care."

"Because she's expecting?"

I said, "Yes."

"Coming here, we lost all four of our girls in one week to
the cholera in Pittsburgh. Rebecca, Ruth, Hannah and Hazel.
Aged two, four, five and seven. And you drink to forget a
babe will be born! Have you no shame?"

Swapped stories at Williams' Tavern with Lambright, Phil,
Jones, and Billy Stump, who said,

"One time, the Randolph folks went to Lewistown for dry
goods, leaving Tim and his sister Betsy to home. Well, now,
Tim, he was fifteen years old, and Betsy about seventeen. It
was a terrible hot day. The boy strips off all his clothes and
lays down on the puncheon floor. Them puncheons was
green ash and shrunk, you see, so a little air come thro' the
cracks. The coolest place in the cabin. Well, pretty soon, the
heat makes Betsy do the same. Off comes her frock and she
lays down naked on the floor, but by the door. Naturally,
tho', they get to talking, and one thing leads to another.
When they're done, Tim rolls off her and says,

" 'My God. How come we never done this before? It's the best I had in my whole life. Hell, you're even better than Ma.'

"His sister, she wriggles her arse, and tells him, 'That's what Pa always says.' "

Phil pulled his butcher knife on him. "I'll cut out your filthy tongue!"

Stump drew his tomahawk.

Jones picked his brass blunderbuss off the bar, primed and cocked it. He said,

"Gentlemen, this piece of mine is loaded with two ounces of buckshot. Put them things away and git. One at a time. Stump first. I mean it, Phil. I'll blow you both to hell. Do what I say. Good. Stump first."

Phil waited five more minutes, like Jones ordered. Never said a word. Soon as he was out the door, Jones asked, "What was all that about?"

Lambright: "Phil's jealous. Martha's sweet on Stump."

29 Oct.

A headache all day, but Lambright was right. I found the compass in the slop bucket.

30 Oct.

Sold here to the Rev. Cooper, 1 lb. cheese......... .10.
       ″   ″   ½ lb. butter .... .15.

The increase during the last year in stiffness of my lower back allows me to dig & haul but 20 lbs. of ginseng roots daily. Nettled by the Rev.'s commiseration. 13 years my senior, he took the tone that we belong to the same generation.

On the other hand, he said that Fanny indeed has an eye for older men—or did before marrying. The jilted Miss Wagner wrote a warning to that effect to Mrs. Cooper.

Accepted the Rev.'s invitation to accompany him & Chapman to a Del. Vision Ceremony (Gam-wing) at Greentown tomorrow eve. He hopes that Armstrong will free the negress. Slightly drunk (10:20 PM). Happy.

1 Nov.
    I have in ready money .... $9.45.

    The Council Lodge, or Long House, made of clapboards & poles, is about 30 ft. wide × 50 ft. long. My eyes still smart from the smoky torches—rolled-up hickory bark. I made out the squaws and warriors seated on opposite sides of the room.
    Montour stood in the middle. I recognized him by the rattlesnake tattooed on his left forearm. He wore a wooden mask, painted red and black; the inlaid copper eyes glittered in the fire light. In his right hand, a rattle made from the shell of a box turtle. In the other, a fan of eagle feathers. He said (according to C.),
    "God has blessed Mak-wa-tut (Little Bear) with a Vision and a Song."
    Little Bear was 12 years old. His voice cracked. He sang something like the following, according to C.:

> Between a hemlock
> And a black rock;
> Hungry, thirsty, sad.
> I sat alone.
> Then the hemlock sang to me.
> He blessed me.
> Now I eat and drink my fill.
> Now I'm glad.

    Tommy Lyons was sleeping it off on the path from the Council House to Armstrong's cabin. C: "His squaw, become an owl, hooted at him in the woods for three hours last night."

1 Nov. ✗ Greentown   78

CHIEF
ARMSTRONG'S
HUT

FOR COUNCILS

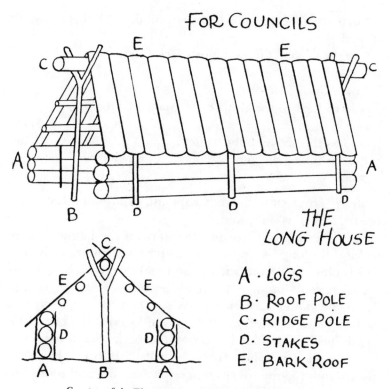

THE
LONG HOUSE

A · LOGS
B · ROOF POLE
C · RIDGE POLE
D · STAKES
E · BARK ROOF

Courtesy of the Thomas Keene Collection, Mansfield, Ohio.

Roasted venison dipped in bear fat mixed with maple sugar, served by Lettiece Shipman. Naked to the waist, black nipples, missing two upper front teeth.

Armstrong told the Rev., "She must serve me till the full moon." (Nov. 30)

C.: "He's waiting on events in Indiana. If Tecumseh whups Harrison, he'll keep her for good."

2 Nov.

Paid to Jacob Beam at his mill for cracking 330 lbs. of my corn, for which I sold him 1 gall., 1 gill, whisky of 80 proof...................................... .33.
.33.

Turned and salted down cheese. Made 30 bullets from lb. of lead.

Diarrhea from Thurs. night's Del. feast.

3 Nov. Sun.

Sold to Levi Jones, at his store, Mans., 10 lbs. cheese.. $1.00.
Sold to the above, 3 lbs. butter .... .90.
Paid in full to the above, 3½ gall. whisky, of 80 proof.

Sharp frost this morn. Chapman, who slept last night before Williams' fire, said,

"Little Bear's song means the Spirit of the hemlock come to him. So long as he lives, this Spirit will provide for him and protect him from witches and bad medicine."

Del. parents indulge a son till he reaches 12 yrs. of age. Then the father slashes the boy's shins with the teeth of a garfish. The mother yells, "I never loved you. Leave! Go away! Die!" She whips him cross the back with a hawthorn branch and drives him from the village into the bush. He must wander alone till God takes pity on him and sends him a Guardian Spirit in a Vision.

Sometimes, nothing happens. The boy is ah-lux-soo. Empty. Like Tommy Lyons. With no Guardian Spirit to protect him. If he stays sober and chaste, observing all the Del. customs, he can try again. He must purge himself and fast for 3 days. Then go into the forest alone, without his weapons, and suffer enough to make God pity him.

4 Nov.

A run of 13½ gall. whisky, of 80 proof from my still.

The diarrhea, gone of its own accord, has left me with bleeding, but painless, piles.

A late Indian summer day. Warm wind from the SE. The fallen leaves give me a view of the sky from the forest floor; my first since the beginning of May.

In his cabin at Greentown, Chief Armstrong wore the tail feathers of a wild turkey as a crown. His skin, dark even for an Indian, inclines me to believe the gossip: he has negro blood.

5 Nov.

At the Coopers' this afternoon. The Rev. seems more melancholy about the continued enslavement of Lettiece Shipman than the death of his son. He said, "Armstrong's getting his revenge. I can't blame him."

The Chief hates Americans. His two sisters—Moravian Christians—were among the 90 Del. massacred at Gnaden-hutten, Ohio, in 1782. The Indians were falsely accused of harboring a Tory spy from Washington County, Penn.

"Them Delaware was pious Christians. They got on their knees, prayed and sang Psalms in Dutch, while a company of 160 Pennsylvania militiamen under Lieutenant-Colonel Williamson beat them to death with mallets and axe handles, then scalped them. Twenty-nine men, twenty-seven women, thirty-four kids, including three babes at the breast. Their heads was smashed against an oak tree on the village green.

"The killing took till sundown—six hours. The Indians begged for mercy. Williamson and his men was drunk.

"They looted and burned the village. Loaded their horses with the spoils and high-tailed it back to Pennsylvania. Had themselves a profitable week. The Dutch beeswax they stole from the church was worth a small fortune by itself."

Fanny said, "What wouldn't I give to have beeswax candles again."

The Rev. asked, "What did you do after Harvard College, Brother Keene?"

"Studied three more years in Cambridge at the Hopkinton Foundation. Then married."

"Studied what?"

"Theology and philosophy."

"And become a pastor."

"Yes."

"Whereabouts?"

"A town on the coast of Maine."

"Till your wife died."

"Till she died."

"What brought you to Richland County, Ohio?"

"Seven years working as a hired hand in Pennsylvania. I wanted a place of my own."

"To start over?"

"To grow old."

He said, "How can you live without Christ?"

"Easily."

"I don't believe you. You write too much in your Journal."

"How do you know that?"

"Since July your fingers are always stained like mine by ink. You got a new callus on the left side, at the first joint, atop the middle finger of your right hand. Only a pen makes that; writing all the time. Not just in a Ledger now and then. No, Brother Keene. You keep a Journal. Want to know why?"

"Yes."

"Being certain you've lost eternal life, you must leave something of yourself behind. I publish bad verse, hoping that a body will read it after I die. I got my doubts about the Resurrection. As Paul says, 'If Christ be not risen, then is our preaching vain and your faith is also vain.' (I Cor. 15:14)."

He has carved on Henry's gravestone:

> Mournfull parents, here I lie.
> As you are now so once was I.
> As I am now, so you will be.
> Prepare for death, and follow me.

On the path back to his cabin, he said, "Armstrong must be under great pressure from Montour to join Tecumseh. But he's a good man. I don't think he'll give in."

Before I left, Fanny asked,

"Have you mentioned me in your Journal, Tom?"

"Often."

"How do you describe the color of my hair?"

"I haven't."

"How would you?"

"The red in it catches the sunlight."

7 Nov.   7:15 PM.

Moved my bowels this morn. without any blood. Chapman is in the barn milking Juno. The Rev. at the well.

We're about to leave for Greentown. C: "The Horned Being (Yak-wa-hey) comes tonight."

8 Nov.

The biggest bear I ever saw burst into the crowded Council House on all fours. Squaws screamed. Then I noticed the pair of antlers on his shaggy brow, and his bushy black tail. Also, his bright red penis, the thickness of my forearm, which dangled almost to the ground. The bear stood up on his hind legs and raised his front paws. His stiff red penis arose as well. The squaws screamed again.

I asked C., "What is he? Man or beast?"

The Rev.: "That's Montour. The old heathen's making himself out to be Yak-wa-hey, the Horned Being—a Devil in charge of folks' health and wild animals. Bucks and squaws will now dance in his honor till dawn, thanking Yak-wa-hey for their good health. The hunters will also ask him to send plenty of game."

9 Nov.
Received here in full from Bob Coffinberry, 16
of his thickest ears of yellow gourdseed corn for
seed.

A new species of maiz, man-made. Coffinberry doesn't question the phenomenon, which he first cultivated 5 or 6 yrs. ago to feed the hogs on his father's farm in Shenandoah County, Va.

It also doesn't bother Chapman, who must make reality jibe with his fancy, or go mad. He admitted as much during our return from Greentown late last night. Told me that a Judge Young of Greensburg, in Westmoreland County, Penn., saved his sanity by introducing him to Swedenborg's Heavenly Doctrine. It explained Beth Holland, who whispers into his left ear.

On Sept. 12, '98, at Young's home, Miss Holland assigned Chapman the task of planting apple trees in the NW Territory. Young, over-joyed by this confirmation of the Heavenly Doctrine, let C. $240 cash without interest for his first nursery—8 acres on Brokenstraw Creek, in Warren County, Penn.

10 Nov. Sun.
Sold to Williams at his Tavern, Mans.,

10 lbs. cheese....................................	.80.
2 lbs. butter....................................	.60.
5 gall. whisky, of 80 proof	1.60.

All cheap at the price, given his profit from the day-long celebration.

Just before sunup, 2 mounted militiamen of the Mt. Vernon Rifles brought news of Harrison's victory over Tecumseh in a battle fought 3 days ago at a place on the Wabash called Tippecanoe. Details are scant, rumors rife.

This afternoon, atop the stump in Central Park, old man Seymour called for our immediate conquest of Canada. The loud applause which followed evoked prolonged, triumphant howls—"Hooooo!"—from Tommy Lyons, and 15 other drunken Del. bucks; they then fired their guns in the air.

13 Nov.
Swapped here with Lambright, 1 pint. whisky of
80 proof, for an apple pie.

He related the following told to him in Mans. last eve. by another mounted militiaman from Mt. Vernon:
Harrison midst the battle on a borrowed horse to a young Kentuckian cocking his piece:
"Where's your captain, son?"
"Dead, sir!"
"Your first-lieutenant?"
"Dead, sir!"
"Your second-lieutenant?"
"Dead, sir!"
"Your ensign?"
"Here, sir!"
This militiaman, named Jethro Stone, also reported that Tecumseh's camp on the Wabash was burned & his host killed or scattered—over 2000 warriors of 11 Nations: Shawanoe, Miami, Ottowa, Chippewa, Kickapoo, Potawatomi,

Sac, Fox, Wyandot & Winnebago. Tecumseh and his brother escaped.

15 Nov.

The dry spell, which allowed me to finish plowing today, is accompanied as usual by smoke from vast forest fires, presently far to the NW.

16 Nov.

Sold to John Chapman, ½ lb. cheese .... .05.
      "   "   , 1 pt. milk...................... .04.

C: "Beth become an angel in Heaven 41 years ago tonight. She says when I die, she'll marry me. I ain't never seen her. She says she has a good figure but a plain face—too big a nose."

17 Nov. Sun.

Sold to Williams, at his Tavern, Mans., 5 gall.
whisky, 80 proof, @ .32...................................... $1.60.

20 Nov. 4 PM.

Rain.

Beginning an hour ago, for the fourth day in a row: nausea, the cold sweats, a dry mouth, pounding heart, shortness of breath. Can't specify the threat.

23 Nov. 4 PM.

Drunk. Rain dripping off grape vines in the bush.

24 Nov. Sun.

Old man Seymour returned to Mans. this morn. from visiting his banker in Chillicothe with the following news:

1. Harrison lost 200 out of 1000 officers & men. They took only 36 scalps—one from a Kickapoo dying in the tall grass after the battle.

2. Tecumseh & his warriors—estimated at about 200 men—have already built a new breastwork of logs about the

ruins of their camp, at the junction of the Wabash & Tippecanoe rivers, 100 miles due N. of Vincennes. Harrison is fortifying the city.

Billy Stump & Martha Seymour strolled hand-in-hand up Main St.; Phil watched.

At Williams' Tavern, Beam explained,

"Martha—that cunt—made Phil swear by the memory of their mother not to raise a rumpus in public."

27 Nov.

Rain all last night; this morn. rainy, foggy, with a gentle S. wind.

Helped Fanny move her things to the Rev.'s cabin, where she & Mrs. Cooper will share the wide rope bed. Their mutual hope for a boy has drawn them together, pleasing the Rev. no end. Sarah said to me,

"The baby might die."

"God forbid," said I.

"There's bound to be trouble either way."

"You sound happy."

"It excites me. I crave excitement."

"So do I."

"I knew it! We got a lot more in common than you and Fanny."

"Why, Sarah Cooper, you're jealous!"

She cried, "Don't flatter yourself," then ran past Fanny, who'd just come inside with an armful of linen.

"Pay the child no heed," she said, glancing at herself in her pocket looking-glass. "What was your poor wife's name, Tom?"

"Abigail."

"How did she die?"

"The bloody flux."

"Was she pretty as me?"

"Not by half."

"Did you love her?"

"No. I was grateful to her for loving me."

"Were you such a sinner?"

"I am a sinful man."

"Ask God's forgiveness."

"I no longer believe in Him. I believe in sin but not God. There's no Savior."

"But that's terrible! Terrible! I pity you."

"I'll take what I can get."

Over dinner—baked acorn squash with molasses & apple pie—the Rev. said, "The Del. won't set foot on my place no more because of Henry's grave by the red cedar. Armstrong's son, Silas, hailed me at the mill today. Very polite, now that Tecumseh's been whupped. His Pa bids me fetch Lettiece Shipman Sat. night at the full moon."

11 PM. One night, about a year after we were married, Abby said to me, "I know you don't love me, Tom. You pity me. I don't mind. I'll take what I can get."

28 Nov.

A hunt at dawn in the wetlands N. of Greentown. 12 men & Bob Coffinberry's pack of 8 Walker hounds. He set the dogs into the swamp. The rest of us covered the likely game paths; I was with the Rev. near the white oak blasted by lightning. The dogs in full cry drove three doe toward us. We killed two. 20 min. later, the Rev. bagged another with his sawed-off rifle.

Bob and George Coffinberry, on horseback, ran down a brown wolf, which came to bay after four hours, his back against a beech tree blown down by the wind. He tore out the throat of a 6 yr. old hound named Rufus, before Bob shot him in the head.

The day's total: 15 deer, 1 bear, a bobcat, 26 turkeys & the wolf.

Sam Lewis, Jr., who was 13 in July, bagged a six-point buck—his first. His Pa cut off the tip of the buck's pecker, which was pink, and handed it to the boy. "Chew that up and swallow it!" Congratulations all around.

The Rev. called him, "Nimrod, a mighty hunter before

the Lord." To me: "What we have taken here today as prey is God's rebuke to Montour and the Del. for their idolatry." My tallow barrel is now full.

29 Nov.

Paid to Jacob Beam for cracking 300 lbs. corn
(my own crop!), for which I sold him 1 gall. less
2 gills whisky, 80 proof......................................   .30.
    .30.

30 Nov.

Declined to accompany the Rev. to Greentown tonight because of a hard rain, presently mixed with sleet. (9 PM).

11 PM. *Masturbatus sum.* The eunuch, who wears gold earrings, is tattooed on his right hip with his mistress's initials—C.P.M.

1 Dec.

I have in ready money .... $6.04.

43 yrs. old today. The sleet has changed to snow.

2 Dec. 9 AM.

Snow.

> Forty three,
> Since yesterday.
> I'm grey,
> Cold,
> And feeling old.

3 Dec.

My wood pile is frozen. (7 AM).
Noon. The sun!

4 Dec.

Fleas in my blankets, mice under the puncheons, & thawing on the hearth since dawn, a 12–14 lb. buck rabbit (*Lepus*); I plucked him by the hind legs from a snow drift near the barn.

2 PM.   The rabbit yawns, stretches his front paws, spreading the toes like a dog. "Rover."

4:15 PM.   Rover breathes more than 240 × a min. Mother kept rabbits; likewise Uncle Joseph at Holden. How could I have forgot that stinking piss?

8 PM.   Rover tried to gnaw a hole in my grain bag. I broke his back with a log.

5 Dec.

> Is Love
> As strong
> As Death?
> I do not know,
> Is Art?
> My Art
> Will raise the part of me
> Writ here
> Within some reader,
> In the year -----
> I do not care.
> This tune,
> This flow:
> Eternity.
>
> (2:20 PM)

6 Dec.
Warmer, the threat of more snow. Dipped candles.

7 Dec.

> Is Love
> As strong
> As Death?
> What of Art?
> I do not know,

But fear
This flow of verse
Will freeze,
And burst
My heart.

(3 PM)

It's either drink or Juvenal.
8 PM. Drunk.

8 Dec. Noon.
Light snow.
A run of 12 gall. whisky, 80 proof.

9 Dec. 7 PM.
Drunk.

10 Dec. 5 AM.
Constipated.
10 PM. Ditto.

11 Dec.
Sold to John Chapman, 40 lbs. dried ginseng
roots, to pay in 1 month .... $5.00.

He refused the stewed rabbit. Miss Holland will reward all
this abstinence in Heaven; their minds will couple there
forever, he says, "begetting innumerable Truths.

"Beth forbade me eat meat at Judge Young's," he said.
"He and I was in the parlor before dinner. The Judge poked
the fire. Beth whispered in my left ear, 'Don't eat the roast
tongue.'

"Now Mrs. Young's roast tongue is famous. The smell
made my mouth water. But I already knowed, don't argue
with Beth. So I nodded. She said, 'Never eat meat again!' "

Black clouds, thunder & lightning made him leave about
4 PM for Beam's mill—2½ miles on snow-shoes, unarmed,

dragging a sled loaded with 150 lbs. of dried ginseng in a staved barrel.

He turns the stuff into a tincture worth $5 a gall.

6 PM. Snow mixed with rain.

11 PM. Slightly drunk. A wolf is barking in the stand of cottonwood cross the creek.

14 Dec.

Gen. Washington died 12 yrs. ago today.

3 PM. Juvenal (eunuch commanded to lick privates).

15 Dec. 5 PM.

Juvenal. Ditto.

16 Dec.

Was spent drunk.

17 Dec. 2 PM.

Off the booze—not a drop—for 8 hrs.

7 PM. Drunk.

19 Dec. 2 PM.

Drunk.

20 Dec.

Drunk.

21 Dec. 4 AM.

Still constipated. Bleeding piles; no pain.

10:50 AM. Cloudy with a brisk N. wind; from 6 AM till ½ hr. ago, heavy snow. Juvenal.

Noon. Drunk. Vomiting.

22 Dec.

Drunk 7 AM.

23 Dec. 11 PM.

Could have froze to death in my stupor last night; the trees cracking from frost, like rifle shots, finally awakened me, after which I took my last drink—one gill at 4 AM.

24 Dec.

Drunk   (4 AM).

1812

----

3 Jan.
Sold to John Lambright, 5 gall. whisky of 80
proof. @ .32.. $1.60.

Monday
January 3, 1812

My Dear Fanny,
   One more favor, I beg you: return this letter. The
Journal in which I will paste it is my hope of Immortality—
as the unborn child is yours.
   That I added the above without fear of offense makes
me very happy. Why hide my thoughts after this past
week? You saw me stupefied with drink. My trembling
tongue spilled water from a cup in your hand. Yes, I
remember. I also recall Sarah half-way up the ladder to
the loft, lantern raised, watching me puke. She retched. I
don't know which is worse—her disgust or your pity.
   The worst is that I owe my life to Chapman, who
brought me to you—and on Christmas Eve!
   Forgive me. Thank you. Have a Happy New Year.
                                                      Tom.

P.S. Beware the negress. She drinks. I smelled it on her
breath last night when you were all asleep.
P.P.S. As you suggested, I've emptied my house of liquor.

5 Jan.
I have in ready money .... $17.64.

This forenoon Phil brought back my letter; returned without comment from Fanny, to whom at dawn he traded 2 rabbits for Henry's red woolen cap.

Phil is the source of Lettiece Shipman's booze, which she hides in the hollow cedar by the grave. Payment (he says with a smirk) for washing & mending his clothes.

Am convinced the smirk means nothing. The man is in love with his sister, but doesn't—I think—yet know. He rants she has lost her honor, i.e., now shares her bed with Stump, who is spending the winter at the Seymour cabin. Their heavy breathing, the rustle of corn husks in her mattress behind a curtain at night—Phil described these twice, while covering his ears. Then he said, "The whore. I'll kill 'em both. Pa too."

He also said, "Montour is dead." And offered me a swig of rum from his canteen.

Montour dead! When? The details escaped me. I was busy keeping my eyes off that canteen.

Phil drinks a pint of booze daily. About my abstinence, he said, "Didn't think you was man enough."

My biggest problem: Idle Hands. Have started a halter. All last night, I plaited hairs plucked from Willy's tail. Thanks (again!) to Chapman, Juno has been with the Rev. since Christmas morn. I miss her.

8 Jan. Wed. 8 PM.
Two weeks without a drink.

9 Jan.
A day of high winds, snow. Drawing map.

12 Jan. 3:30 PM.
> ". . . play
> With it.
> Try what you may.

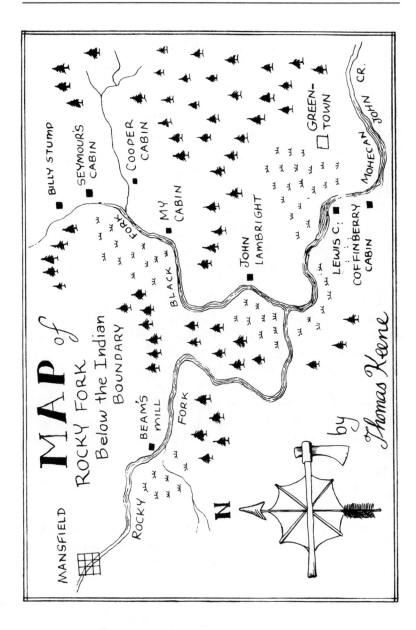

Courtesy of the Thomas Keene Collection, Mansfield, Ohio.

It will stay
Wrinkled & limp."
                                    Martial, XI., 47.

13 Jan.   6:30 PM.
Cloudy, with a hard NW. wind. On the way back just now
from the barn—125 yds.—the cold made my eyes water,
froze the hair in my nostrils.

13 Jan.
Able to sleep only after sunup.

15 Jan.   Mon.   11 PM.
3 wks. without a drink. Off my feed all day.

16 Jan.
The start of a Jan. thaw. Lambright here, puffing on a
cigar. We supped on a loaf of black walnut corn bread & a
pt. of buttermilk—gifts from his wife.
About my abstinence, he said, "I'm glad." Also, "I envy
you."
About his glimpse last Sat. of Miss Shipman, he remarked,
"What folks say is true. Negroes are proof that Indians fuck
buffaloes." Then he added, "It's good hearing you laugh
again."
Martial (9 PM).

17 Jan.
This morn.'s fog restricts my vision to 15–20 ft. But what
sounds! Sparrows chirp, the running water tinkles under the
ice on the creek. Not for Henry Cooper.

18 Jan.
Leased to the Rev. till 1 Jan. 1814, 1 calf's
stomach, preserved by salt, & Juno, for which
he owes me in the interim to pay on the 1st

Inst., ½ of any profit he makes by selling dairy produce. If Juno dies on or before the aforesaid date, he or his heir owes me to pay on the 1st Inst., her hide, horns, hooves, offal & rendered fat.

The above are the conditions under which he finally agreed to keep her. When Fanny said, "Dearest Tom," Mrs. Cooper gasped.

At supper, Fanny told me,

"Night before last—I swear—Pa slammed the door shut and the baby jumped. You think it possible he hears in the womb?"

19 Jan.

Checked the mill today; it's running. Beam told me that Montour didn't die of pneumonia, as he had prophesied. "The dysentery took him. I got nothing to worry about."

20 Jan.   A rainy Sun.

Paid in full to Jacob Beam for cracking 330 lbs. my corn, for which I sold him 15 lbs. ground meal .... .33.

.33.

Declined a drink with breakfast—Ma's Johnny cakes & honey. She yelled,

"If you don't lay off that stuff yourself, you old fool, you'll be dead within the year, like Montour foretold."

"Shut your mouth, woman!"

21 Jan.   9 PM.

A soft wet snow has been falling since I returned at 4 o'clock from the Coopers', where Fanny lies abed—heartburn. She's attended by Lettiece, whose breath no longer smells of booze.

"A drunken man does what a sober man thinks," said she to me. "I can't afford to drink."

What would owning such a woman feel like?

Juno is in good hands. The Rev. has already discovered she enjoys being scratched under the chin.

His wife resents that Henry's last words were for Fanny. Viz.,

"After I'm dead, I mean to come back and set round on the stumps and watch you and see how you're getting along. See if I don't."

22 Jan. Noon.

Froze hard last night; sunny all morn. 1 month since taking a drink.

3 PM. Martial.

11 PM. Martial.

23 Jan.

Cloudy, warmer; wind SSW.

24 Jan.

Snow changed this afternoon to rain; wind S. westerly.

25 Jan.

Rain all day. At dusk, snow.

26 Jan.

Am indebted to pay Lettiece Shipman here on demand, 1 pt. whisky for washing my clothes.

As the water boiled, she sang (with a lisp caused by her missing front teeth),

> Our father, who is in heaven,
> White man owe me eleven
> But pay me seven.
> Thy kingdom come,
> Thy will be done.
> If I hadn't took that,
> I wouldn't have none.

27 Jan.
Throughout this warm night, a horned owl has been hooting for a mate. "Whoo-whoo-whoooooo-whoo-whoo." (The prolonged note has the lowest pitch.)

30 Jan. 12:30 PM.
Martial.

1 Feb.
I have in ready money .... $17.64.

3 Feb.
Received in full from John Chapman, for
ginseng roots .... $5.00.

He is snoring on the floor before my fire. Tomorrow, we go to Greentown so I can paint Tommy Lyons' portrait with a set of Windsor Newton water colors which the former bought ($3.50) for the occasion in Mt. Vernon.

"Tommy Lyons has had a vision. God worked a miracle thro' me," said C. He wears four pairs of pants.

4 Feb.
Trip postponed—heavy snow. C., who's fetching fire wood, said that on Fri. morn., Dec. 27th, outside Williams' Tavern, Miss Holland whispered, "Montour's with me."

"I got myself to Greentown fast," said C. "Sure enough, the great medicine man was dead. Montour! Why, he could calm the north wind. I seen him do it.

"The ground was froze solid so we buried him in an abandoned storage pit. I asked Beth, 'Now what?' And Proverbs 29:18 popped into my head: 'Where there is no vision the people perish.' "

The upshot? With C.'s help, Tommy Lyons has acquired a mighty guardian Spirit & taken up his late father's trade. A week ago yesterday, he healed a boil on Chief Armstrong's neck by waving an eagle feather over it.

C.: "I must not reveal more."

5 Feb.

No trip today, either. About 10 inches of snow has fallen. Must prop up the roof-ribs of my cabin & barn. C. will cut timber.

7 PM.   Chapman wagged his tongue all afternoon.

Item: Tommy Lyons sobered up to attend his dying father at the latter's request.

Item: When he had mourned the obligatory 12 days, then fasted 36 hrs. & purged himself, Lyons asked Chapman's help in his quest for a guardian Spirit.

Said C., "First I told him what he—and every Delaware—already knows. 'Make God pity you.' Then I added something on my own; a divine inspiration! 'Go and suffer all you feel about your Pa,' I said. 'Your grief, love, hate. Suffer your hate, especially. That will break God's heart. I know from experience.'

"Well, sir, off he goes, out of the Council House, into the soft snow. It was about 3 o'clock in the morning. The north wind covered his tracks. He went straight to the hollow red cedar by Henry Cooper's grave. That took great courage. The Delaware believe the Spirit of the sacred tree is angry—very dangerous—because of the grave. Lyons said it started snowing very hard.

"On the south side of that tree is a big hole. Lyons crawled in. The hollow was dry, about three feet in diameter, and high enough for him to stand up. All about was lots of soft, rotten wood. He crawled back out, stripped naked, save for his moccasons, lest they freeze, and buried his breech-clout and leggins in his Hudson Bay coat under a rock. Then, with his tomahawk, he fell to chopping at the top of a fallen hemlock that lay near, and piled the wood against the hole till it was three or four feet thick—except at one spot. He stopped that with a block he hauled after him.

"Once inside, by the dim light, he chopped down all the rotten wood he could, beat it small, and made a round bed, like a goose nest. That's where he buried his moccasons. Then he danced in the center to get warm. Meanwhile, the snow had sealed him up. It was dark as the grave. He squatted there thinking about his Pa. Not like us whites knowed him—as Montour—but as 'Nee-kah-pah-nox-way.' 'He who stalks before dawn.' The great Del. medicine man.

"Lyons rocked back and forth. Finally, he made up a song that goes something like this:

> Father!
> When I was empty,
> You was full.
> But now—Ka-yah!

"That there's an exclamation of wonder. 'Ka-yah!' He stood up, arms over his head, and sang:

> Father!
> When I was empty,
> You was full.
> Now I fill this tree,
> And worms fill you!

"Next, bit by bit, he chewed a handful of the rotten wood, swallowed it, and sang:

> Father!
> When I was empty,
> You was full.
> Now I eat this tree,
> And worms eat you!

"His spirit left his body, which turned black and putrid. His jaw bone fell off; also both arms. His legs broke at the knees. He had a vision of a rattlesnake. Then a female Spirit picked up his bones and put them back together. He cried out,

" 'Ka-yah! I'm alive again! All in one piece! Thank you, Spirit, for pitying me. Who are you?'

"She sang, 'I'm every thing there is, was and will be. The fruit I have borne is the sun.'

"He said, 'Ka-yah! Lucky me! My Guardian Spirit is Ka-ha-suna—Our Mother, the earth.' "

6 Feb.

This morn. proved fair. Finished propping the roof-ribs of my barn about 5 PM. Then an easy ride over the dry snow to Greentown, where Chapman is called En-naughk (My father). Chief Armstrong spread a bearskin for us to sit upon in his cabin. 2 squaws served me boiled beaver tail—tender with a woody taste—& C. mush. No booze.

At Lyons' command, the punishment for drunkenness among these people—including kids—is being burned alive. A stake has been erected for this purpose near the W. door of the Council House.

A meager supper of parched corn. Chapman & I lodge tonight with Armstrong and the afore-mentioned squaws— a mother and her 14 yr. old daughter—who are his wives. The girl, who tends the fire in the center of the earthen floor, has a bad cough; the smoke eventually makes its way out thro' a hole in the roof.

Re fires: Lyons keeps one burning atop Montour's grave to drive off wolves.

C. says that after being washed, richly painted & dressed, a Del. corpse is buried in a coffin with a perforated lid so the Spirit can escape.

7 Feb.

An exhausting day's work, at the very end of which I solved my toughest problem—the fringed hood on Lyons' coat—with a pair of Armstrong's scissors & some paste. Early this morn., he killed a doe. His squaws extracted the marrow from the shank bones; broke, then boiled them for the grease they smear on their plaited hair.

Am sure Armstrong is part negro. He has not, however, asked after Miss Shipman.

He did say that Lyons indeed brought his boil to a head with an eagle feather—plus a hot poultice of corn flour.

Courtesy of the Thomas Keene Collection, Mansfield, Ohio.

8 Feb.

"I hereby certify that this portrait of Kanotchy (The Wild Cat), a Delaware Medicine Man also called Tommy Lyons, was painted from life, at Greentown, on the Black Fork Creek, Richland County, Ohio, in the year 1812, by Thomas Keene. (Signed) John Chapman."

C. wrote the above on the back of my painting late this afternoon.

Lyons and Armstrong took one look at the former's likeness & clapped their left hands over their open mouths— the Indian gesture of amazement, says C. He waited till we were alone to translate Armstrong's exclamation, " 'No Delaware medicine man ever accomplished such a feat!' " Explaining why Lyons stalked out.

"Armstrong's jealous of him," said C. "The old fool is consumed with self-love."

And I by fleas, infesting my borrowed blanket.

7 PM. Supped again on parched corn. Afterwards, C. & I smoked a foul pipe with Armstrong. He wants to swap the girl & his scissors for my watch.

9 Feb.

Home since noon. Chapman, who remained as Lyons' guest, refused my offer of the portrait, saying,

"Hold out your right hand and tell me what you see."

"The nails want paring."

Said he, "You got a short memory. Less than a month ago, it shook so bad you couldn't bring a cup of water to your mouth. Keep the painting, Brother Keene. Look at it whenever you crave a drink."

I am.

10 Feb.

Mrs. Lambright, puffing on a cigar, came over with breakfast—a loaf of pumpkin bread. She said the Rev. will signal the onset of Fanny's labor by firing 2 shots atop the bluff.

11 PM. Martial.

11 Feb.

Killed a buck at dawn on the deer run cross the creek but was prevented from dressing the skin by a sudden rain.

The rest of the day, I killed fleas.

12 Feb.

Very cold. Repaired the garden fence.

13 Feb. Thurs. 7:20 AM.

2 shots!

10 AM. Awaiting news with Sarah, Lambright & Beam in Fanny's old cabin; thro' the window by the door, I can just make out the red cedar's charred trunk. Sarah says,

"Pa set it afire. Last Monday, Lettiece found an Indian sign carved in the bark facing Henry's grave and showed Ma. What a shriek! I heard her in the loft. 'The Mark of the Beast!' "

"What did it look like?"

"Gimme five cents and I'll draw you a picture in your Ledger."

"Two."

"For making a graven image? That's a mortal sin. Three. Not a penny less."

"I owe you three cents."

Said she, "Don't tell my folks. Promise?"

"You have my word."

"Hand me your pen."

She says Elizabeth was her late sister's name; she died 15 yrs. ago, aged 5, of intermittent fever.

She also said, "My brother Arnold was strangled at birth by his own cord. I was only four, but you wouldn't believe how much I recollect. He was blue. One blue little arm flopped back and forth when Pa picked him up."

12:20 PM. Mrs. Lambright reports Fanny took some toast & water, & half a cup of thin gruel.

Jones, Mrs. Lewis, Bob Coffinberry & his brother George's

The Mark of the Beast

by
Sarah Elizabeth Cooper

wife have arrived. Also the Seymours, save Phil, who's checking his trap lines along the Rocky Fork. Martha looks the same; her father's beard is all white. When Jones asked about his winter wheat, he called out, "Billy!"

Martha said, "You told Billy to stay home and mend the roof, Pa."

12:30 PM. Williams is here with a ½ gall. keg of rum.

1 PM. From Lettiece, who fixed dinner: "Pains are sharper. Nothing to fret about yet."

The smell of baked beans & hot bread—whole wheat! Lambright, Coffinberry, Beam already drunk. The Rev. is reading his Bible by the window. Sarah has whispered in my ear, "Lettiece has told Pa what the Indian sign means."

Says Lettiece, "Meet me in the barn with a jug."

3:15. She said, "You still owes me a pint for washing your clothes.

"About this sign. It's the Great Spirit's pecker. Miss Sarah drawed too many eyes; should have only six on each side. They never would tell me why. Said one winter when there weren't no game, the Great Spirit Ke-tahn-it-too-weet lived on gum bark a whole month. He took ahold of his bow and reed arrows, saying, 'Maybe today my luck will change.'

"Sure enough, a hundred paces from his lodge, he come upon deer tracks in the deep snow and followed 'em. Now the snow, it had a thin crust. Even tho' Ke-tahn-it-too-weet was wearing snow-shoes, he kept breaking thro'. But he figured that deer up yonder was having trouble too. He followed them tracks all day. Just before sundown, he spied a doe browsing on twigs midst a stand of sugar trees.

"Ke-tahn-it-too-weet's pecker got stiff. Being mighty curious, it said, 'I want a look at the doe.'

" 'Set back down,' says Ke-tahn-it-too-weet. 'You're so long I can't draw my bow.'

"His pecker said, 'First let me look at the doe.'

"Ke-tahn-it-too-weet said, 'The crust on the snow is froze solid. Any second now, that doe will bolt. Do what you're told. Set down so's I can draw my bow.'

"His pecker said, 'No.' Ke-tahn-it-too-weet reached under his breech-clout, grabbed tight, yanked his pecker off, and throwed it over his shoulder. The snow melted for miles around. Flowers bloomed. Ke-tahn-it-too-weet killed the doe. His pecker, it turned into the first rattlesnake. Whether Ke-tahn-it-too-weet growed another, I can't say."

3:45 PM. Beam, to whom I owe the jug, has learned from his wife that Fanny broke water late last night; she must endure a dry birth.

4:15 PM. Mrs. Lambright again: for the past hour, Fanny's pains have been coming every 10 min.

Williams just cracked his keg of rum.

5:45 PM. Which drove me outside. Unable to see thro' the Coopers' frosted window, I turned away; Fanny yelled, "Somebody help me!"

Fed and watered Willy & Juno in the crowded barn. On my way back, as I came abreast of the door, Fanny screamed. Lettiece said something unintelligible. Mrs. Cooper replied,

"I never heard such nonsense. Your drunkenness is bad enough. Hold your tongue or else!"

"Yes'm."

"Now get rid of that filth and slice the venison."

"Yes'm."

Fanny cried, "Why don't nobody help me?"

6:30 PM. Cold venison, mashed potatoes, & bread pudding, courtesy of Lettiece, who muttered, "Mrs. Cooper, she too stupid to be white. Ever seed a woman give birth then bleed to death, Mr. Keene?"

Coffinberry called, "More bread pudding, gal."

He told me, "I bet she meant to stuff Fanny up inside with a handful of soot and cobwebs. Aunty Claire, who belonged to Doc Skinner at Heartland, done the same; owned it prevents bleeding. It don't."

7:15 PM. Raining hard.

8:43 PM. The first white baby born in Richland County is a healthy 6 lb. 10 oz. girl; Fanny well. Sarah weeps.

9:10 PM. Before Coffinberry could stop her, Lettiece threw the after-birth, wrapped in her apron, onto the fire—another preventative of hemorrhage.

9:50 PM. Fanny is calling for me.

10 PM. She asked, "Where's Johnny at, Tom? Do you know?" I answered, "No." Going home.

14 Feb.
Bleeding piles.

15 Feb.
Bought of Levi Jones, at his store, Mans., 3
steel pens @ .01 .... .03.
Bought of Levi Jones, 4 oz. India ink .... .04.
Bought of Levi Jones, for my paintings, 1 Extra
Large Post size pasteboard map case, with cloth
handles .... .50.
Bought of Levi Jones, 1 ivory comb .... .30.
Bought of Williams at his tavern, 1½ qt. whisky,
which I owe to repay in kind on demand.
Paid in full to Bob Coffinberry, at his forge on
Diamond St., for sharpening my ploughshare, 1
pt. whisky.
Paid in full to Jacob Beam, at his mill, 1 qt.
whisky.

Beam told me that if the weather holds, Fanny's daughter will be baptized tomorrow noon, sponsored by Mrs. Lambright & himself.

"I was Fanny's second choice. She'd already asked Chapman, but about two hours after you left, he showed up, mentioned being at Greentown, and Mrs. Cooper slammed the door in his face. Nor would she say why. Fanny cried.

Me, a godfather! The Reverend filled me in. It's a grave responsibility. I'd no idea."

16 Feb. Sun. eve.
Paid in full to Sarah Cooper .... .03.

Beam stayed sober; Chapman wasn't there. Carrie Grace Cooper, named after her late maternal grandmother, has inherited Henry's shapely hands.

Lettiece bathes Fanny's piles thrice daily with a cloth wrung out of warm water. "The surest cure."

Fanny: "I'm grateful to God for the pain, Tom. I'm a monster. I don't feel no love for Carrie, even when I give her suck."

17 Feb.
The fine weather continues. Bleeding piles, but no pain. Killed a beaver for his skin & tail, on which I supped.

18 Feb.
This morn. passed a big clot of blood with my stool.

19 Feb.
Not a drop today. Spite Lettiece's fomentations, Fanny's piles are excruciating. She thanked me for my gift to Carrie of the ivory comb, & said, "Come back tomorrow, Tom."

20 Feb. 3 PM.
She said, "These last weeks, I've been reading Swedenborg's book again, Tom. Suppose he's right? That means Henry's now judging himself. It says here in Chapter 57, 'No one is cast into Hell by the Lord; this is done by the Spirit himself.' Is Henry in Hell? I got to know.

"Fetch Johnny here, Tom. Make peace between him, Ma and Pa. He speaks with an angel called Beth; she promised to tell him if Henry be saved or damned."

21 Feb. 1 PM.
Caught in a downpour while returning from Williams'
Tavern, Mans. Chapman hasn't slept there in over 2 weeks.
Phil, at the bar, said,
"This is the time of the year Johnny tends his nursery on
Owl Creek. Come Saturday, I'll be out that way myself, to
Mt. Vernon. Any message?"
"I must speak with him about Fanny."
2 PM. Martial.

22 Feb.
Ploughed all day. About 4 o'clock, I glanced behind me.
Perched atop a clod of earth, a small (male?) horned owl
snatched a mouse from the fresh furrow & flew off with it
in his beak to the hemlock near the creek.

23 Feb. 7 AM.
I was right—a male. The female is almost twice his size.
They devoured a rabbit together just now in the hemlock.
1 PM. Finished ploughing; owls gone. Chapman is at the
door.

24 Feb.
C. looked at Sarah's drawing & cried out, "On that tree,
you say? Facing the grave? God above! What news!"
We rode to the Coopers', where he said,
"Sometime round sunup, January 9th, Tommy Lyons seen
Henry's Spirit at the grave. The sign he carved means, 'a
male Spirit come here from God.' I tell you—Tommy Lyons
seen Henry's Spirit; maybe they spoke. Shall I try to find
out?"
Mrs. Cooper said, "Yes. After breakfast, tomorrow.
Do so."
The Rev. kept mum. Fanny thanked me for bringing this
about. "I'm so happy, Tom. God has opened my heart. I
love my babe."

25 Feb.
Cold & rainy.

26 Feb.
Sold to Levi Jones, at his store, Mans., 1½ lb.
beaver skin, for which he paid me in full .... $2.00.
Bought of Levi Jones, 1 pair harness needles .....   .15.
Bought of Levi Jones, 1 spool waxed linen
harness thread ....   .25.
Bought ½ lb. salt ....   .50.
Bought ¼ lb. refined cane sugar ....   .25.
Bought ½ lb. young hyson tea ....   .72.

27 Feb.
A cup of green tea with 3 spoonfuls of sugar! Cold &
cloudy all day. Mended bridle.

28 Feb.   Fri.   6 AM.
Clear & pleasant. Off to Mans. with Lettiece, who arrived
here afoot. She says Fanny's piles are much improved. No
news of Chapman since he left the Coopers for Greentown,
Wed. morn.

11 PM.
Bought of Williams, at his tavern, Mans., 1 pt.
whisky ....   .07.
Paid there in full to Lettiece Shipman for
washing my clothes, 1 pt. whisky.

She said, "I'se barren.
"Five years ago, at potato time, the middle of July, Massa
Smith bid me breed. Frank, the brick-yard hand, fucked me
first. He wore an iron collar with one link of chain. After
him was Ben, the waiting boy, then Ned. Massa, he said,
'Frank, try again.'
"When nothing come of that, Massa yelled, 'You barren
bitch!' and punched me in the mouth. Knocked out my front

teeth. I was cried off to Massa Sloat for three hundred dollars in Lewisburg the following month."

29 Feb.

Bought this morn. of Williams, at his tavern,
Mans., 1 pt. whisky .... .07.

11:15 PM. *Masturbatus sum.*

Self-Love.

2 swigs
Plus what
I've writ above
Of her
Have raised me up again.

5:30 PM. Drunk.

1 March.

I have in ready money .... $23.47.

2 March.

Received here in full from the Rev. Cooper, ½
of his profit from his sale of dairy produce .... $2.63.

He said, "Johnny's crazy. Tommy Lyons worships Satan. But I couldn't refuse Ma. She misses Henry so. God won't forgive me for trafficking with evil spirits."

3 March.

Bought of Levi Jones at his store, Mans., 4
yards of shirting cotton, @ 50 ¢ .... 2.00.
Bought 1 spool white thread .... .20.
Bought 2 sleeve buttons .... .03.
Bought 1 pair short stockings............................. .50.

Jones has kept a grocery in his cabin opposite Williams' Tavern on the corner of Main St. & Park Ave. W. for 3 years. He plans to clear off a place about ½ mile E. of town for a brickyard. A confirmed bachelor, short with female customers. The brick business will suit him better.

He put his jug upon the counter between us, saying, "Williams tells me you're back on the booze."

"I knew he would."

"Look at my tongue. I puke first thing every morning. My liver's shot. Save yourself. Leave the jug be. Good man!"

4 March.

Abby died 8 yrs. ago today.

5 March.

This morn. rainy. Finished shirt.

7 March.

Helped the Lambrights open 50 of their sugar trees.

8 March.

Boiled 30 lbs. sugar at the Lambrights' till midnight. Why did they not have more kids after their girls died? I sense they are content with each other.

10 March. Tues. eve.

Chapman here late this afternoon on his way to the Coopers'. He said,

"Tommy Lyons won't say if he met Henry's spirit. Ka-ha-suna won't allow it. Guardian Spirits are tetchy."

11 March.

Was spent at the Coopers'. Nobody mentioned Chapman. I daubed Fanny's old cabin, into which she, Carrie & Lettiece have moved. Chimney & roof in good shape. The place already smells of soiled napkins & sour milk. Fanny's breasts are now as big as Martha Seymour's!

The baby awakens to be nursed every 3 hrs. Fanny: "She's a good eater. It figures. She was born with a callus on her right thumb. Sucked it in the womb. Beautiful, ain't she? She got my Pa's eyes."

12 March. 9:45 AM.
Rain mixed with snow.

13 March.
Paid this morn. at the mill in full to Ma Beam 2 lbs. meal for grinding 60 lbs. my corn .... .06.
.06.

Jacob, who was abed, said, "I done it; quit cold. Ain't touched a drop since the night before Carrie got baptized. No, that's my pride's talking, sinner that I am. It was God done it; Him and the Reverend's prayers pulled me thro'. Ask Ma."
She said, "The Reverend dosed him with laudanum; that's what stopped his fits."

14 March. 7 PM.
Heavy rain with thunder & lightning.

15 March. Sun. eve.
Paid in full this morn. to Bob Coffinberry, at his forge, Mans., for shoeing Willy .... .50.
Paid in full to Williams, at his Tavern, for supper .... .10.

War? "The Chillicothe Independent Republican" reports that in Jan. Congress voted to recruit 25,000 more men for the Regular Army & raise a militia of 50,000 volunteers. The law, however, doesn't specify if said militia can be used outside the Country—i.e., to invade Canada. Even some War Hawks argue this violates the Constitution; militia can legally be used only for home defense. Where does it say that? Poor Madison must be tearing his hair.

16 March. 5 AM.
A blustering N. wind; snow.
7:30 PM. Spite the continuing snow storm, Chapman wouldn't stay over night. Tommy Lyons has invited us back to Greentown immediately the weather clears.
Said C., "Something's up. I don't know what."

17 March.
Snow with some rain.

18 March.
Chapman and I at Greentown this morn. There were Wyandot, Ottowa & Shawanoe warriors among the three to four hundred Indians from all parts of northern Ohio gathered outside the Council House. Tommy Lyons addressed them, saying (C.'s translation),
"Dear Brothers, I want to die."
One by one, 19 half-naked young Del. warriors stepped forward & repeated the same words. Like Tommy Lyons, each held in his left hand a bow & a barbed red arrow. They then formed into 2 rows of 10, opposite one another, at 20 yds. Tommy Lyons, who was facing me, whooped; all drew their bows overhead. He whooped again & they shot the arrows straight up. Everybody watching, including C. & I, ran for cover. The two of us took shelter in the Council House doorway. The bucks never moved.
Their barbed red arrows rose about 175 feet, stopped dead, fell backwards, then gradually turned over. The warriors—arms folded—were all looking up when the arrows dropped among them. A young buck on the end of the row to my left toppled back. The arrow thro' his left eye came out behind his right ear. His blood melted a patch of snow. An old squaw threw herself on the corpse.
C. & I lit out on Willy. Near the white oak blasted by lightning, he cried, "My God!" & "Beth!" Then, "What have I done?"

He continued on snow-shoes to Mans.; I rode to the Coopers'. The Rev. said,

"Keep calm. Chief Armstrong wants peace. I'm to meet with him on the Sabbath. His son, Silas, brung me the message yesterday. 'Come, let us reason together.' That was his Pa's word: 'reason'—'Pe-nau-a-lin.'

"Don't spread panic and strengthen Tommy Lyons' hand. Forbear. Say nothing. Leastways, not till I've heard Armstrong out. Come with me, then decide."

"I will."

He has bought a 2 yr. old no-account spotted bitch named Pru, from Bob Coffinberry for $1.50. A pet for Sarah, of whom he (the Rev.) said, "She's lonely."

19 March.
The sun has melted the snow.

20 March.
Another fine day with a brisk SE wind; aired my goods & scrubbed the floor.

21 March. 7 PM.
Ploughed & tilled since dawn.

22 March. Sun. 11 AM.
In the Council House, Greentown, where Armstrong is making a speech. His audience—warrior & squaw alike—frequently sobs. Tommy Lyons is seated cross-legged on the earthen floor to my left.

It looks like the Rev. was right: there is no cause for panic. The Ottowas, Wyandots & Shawanoes have gone.

2 PM.   Armstrong said in effect that this month marks the 30th anniversary of the massacre by Americans of 90 Del. Christians—Moravian Brethren—at Gnadenhutten. "They who renounced the ways of our forefathers"—the converts—

"were taught to plant vegetables, grow fruit trees, & raise cattle, horses & hogs. Their cabins were lit by beeswax candles. A brass bell summoned them to worship Jesus Christ. Their children studied the Bible."

To the Rev.: "The twenty-eight children were brained with hatchets; their parents were forced to watch. They knelt in the mud, praising the white man's God, who forbade them to fight back."

He declared, "Jesus Christ and whisky (pronounced 'whish-kee')—tricks of the whites! Worship Ke-tahn-it-too-weet!" (He Who Created Us By His Thought—the Great Spirit). "Do not drink whisky any more!"

He also said, "The Chiefs of our Nation pledged themselves at Greene Ville to keep the peace. I was there with the great medicine man, Nee-kah-pah-nox-way (Montour); we took the oath together, on our honor as warriors. Tecumseh wants me to break my oath & make war. I will not. Nee-kah-pah-nox-way's son asks, 'How can you trust white people?' I never have. If my village is attacked, I will fight. But I will not go back on my word."

The Rev. tore his shirt down the front, exposing his flabby breast, & replied,

"Kill me, I beg you by Jesus Christ, if ever your village is attacked by whites."

Armstrong yelled, "Amen!"

They shook left hands, Indian fashion.

Tommy Lyons said, "Tecumseh bids us join with him & drive the whites from our country once & for all. You know he is right, but you are afraid. I see it on your faces. Fear also Roaring Wing's angry Spirit. He shed his blood for you in vain."

23 March.

Ploughed & tilled till noon. A dinner of muskrat stew at the Lambrights'. They are moved by the Rev.'s oath.

Lambright: "His life is safe with us. But he best beware of Tommy Lyons."

A scandal yesterday at Williams' Tavern. Billy Stump refused to pay the 17 ¢ postage due on a letter from his wife in Cincinnati, saying, "Martha's my true love."

26 March.

I take back what I wrote about Pru. She gave Sarah & me a close look at a horned owl's nest today. The hound's barking attracted our attention to an overturned beech near the spring. Sarah spotted the nest—5 ft. from the ground— midst the tangled roots. It stinks of rotten meat. 2 young owls but a little larger than newly hatched chickens. Covered with white down, eyes shut, unable to hold up their heads, they nestle in 2 half-eaten rabbits.

Whenever Carrie (age 6 wks.) is laid upon her back, she turns her head to her right, then raises her rt. forearm. The blister on her upper lip is gone. Lettiece is treating Fanny's chapt nipples with cool purges. The latter said, "We've become friends." She has the bluest eyes.

27 March. Good Friday.

A run of 13 gall. whisky. 80 proof, from my Still.

28 March. 11 PM.

Haven't touched a drop. Chapman is Fanny's guest, according to Mrs. Lambright, who bought cheese of the Rev. early this afternoon.

29 March. Easter Sunday.

What follows almost verbatim is the sermon delivered by the Rev. at dawn from atop the white oak stump in Central Park:

" 'And if Christ be not risen, then is our preaching vain & your faith is also vain.' 1 Cor. 15:14.

"The Apostle Paul hits the nail on the head. Did Christ rise from the dead today or not? I say, 'Yes. He did!' John is the witness who convinces me. Listen how he describes himself & Peter in John, Chap. 20, Verses 4–7:

" 'So they ran both together, and the other disciple did outrun Peter and came first to the sepulchre. And he stooping down & looking in, saw the linen clothes lying, yet went he not in. Then cometh Simon Peter, following him, and went into the sepulchre, & seeth the linen clothes lie. And the napkin, that was about his head, not lying with the linen clothes but wrapped together in a place by itself.'

"Being younger than Peter, John outruns him; he stoops at the entrance to the tomb, sees them linen clothes, but don't go in. How come? Think! Because he's thunder-struck at the sight—burial clothes in a heap on the floor! Meanwhile, Peter pushes past. He spots not only the clothes, but that napkin, 'wrapped together in a place by itself.'

"What's so important about that? Think again! Think again! Jesus kept Himself neat. That's common sense. Picture it. After rising from the dead, He wraps up the napkin, and puts it in a place by itself. How like Him!

"That's why John then tells us in Verse 8,

" 'Then went in also that other disciple, which came first to the sepulchre, and he saw, & believed.'

"Sure he did. So do I. 'I believe in God the Father Almighty, Maker of Heaven & Earth; & in Jesus Christ, His only Son Our Lord; who was conceived by the Holy Spirit, born of the Virgin Mary, suffered under Pontius Pilate, was crucified, dead, & buried; the 3rd day He rose from the dead; He ascended to Heaven & sitteth at the right hand of God the Father Almighty; from thence He shall come to judge the quick & the dead. I believe in the Holy Spirit; the Holy Catholic Church, the Communion of Saints, the for- giveness of sins, the resurrection of the body & the life everlasting.' That wrapped up napkin clinches it for me."

30 March.
   Paid in full to Williams at his tavern, Mans.,
   1½ qt. whisky, 80 proof.
   Bought this morn. of Jones, at his store,
   Mans., 3 sheets of Royal size drawing paper
   @ .03 ....   .09.
   Bought 2 sticks, India ink, @ 11 ¢ ....   .22.
   Bought 4 oz. white lead ....   .025.

   Swapped him my spectacles for a stronger pair.

1 April.
   I have in ready money .... $23.445.

3 April.
   Received in full from the Rev., ½ his monthly
   profit from the sale of dairy produce ....   .61.

   One month since my last drink.
   The Rev. & I rode to Greentown. I showed my painting
to Tommy Lyons. The Rev. translated my explanation, Viz.,
   "This is Our Mother who revealed Herself to me thro' 2
horned owl chicks nesting midst the roots of an overturned
beech near the Rev.'s spring."
   Tommy Lyons clapped his left hand over his mouth. Then
he sat down, cross-legged on a bearskin, and stared at the
painting for an hour, smoking his pipe.

4 April.
   Sold to John Lambright, 1 pt. whisky, 80 proof .....   .04.

   He's heard Phil now lives in Stump's old cabin but retains
half interest in the profits from his father's Still.

5 April   7:30 PM.
   Finished cross ploughing.

Courtesy of the Thomas Keene Collection, Mansfield, Ohio.

6 April.
Tilled all day.

7 April.
Ditto.
I first met Fanny a year ago today in Central Park at about 10:30 in the morn. She wore her brown cloak—spattered with mud. Her Roman nose ravished me.

9 April.
The young owls have changed from white to dirty brown. Pale yellow eyes. They nestle among bones & a fox's skull. The side of their nest, which has been beaten down, is slimy from excrement—whitish, flecked with black specks.
Carrie has a cold.
Fanny doesn't remember our first meeting.

10 April.
Ploughed till rain started (2 PM).

11 April. 7:30 PM.
Damnable Ohio sod! Must plough & till again.

12 April.
Paid in full to Bob Coffinberry at his forge,
Diamond St., Mans., for steeling & sharpening
my knife coulter, 1 pint whisky, 80 proof...........   .04.
                                                          .04.

Which he swapped with a young Del. buck, called Toby, for a prime beaver skin worth $2.00.

17 April. Sat. eve.
Ploughing & tilling done.

18 April.
This day spent in Mans. with Fanny. She was 3 when her
mother died. An only child. She invented an invisible play-
mate—"Scamper." Her father made scabbard belts, shoes &
cartridge boxes for the Army during the Revolution, & built
a house on Market St. in Harrisburg, where he died when
Fanny was 13.
"The worst thing that's happened to me."
She then lived with an uncle, aunt & 5 cousins on a farm
between Harrisburg and Dauphin.
9:30. *Masturbatus sum.* (Fanny).

19 April.
This morn. Fanny agreed to marry me before the year is
out; we will keep our betrothal secret till after the anniversary
of Henry's death.
"Henry was a baby. I hanker for someone to depend on.
An older man. That's you, Tom."
Abby loved me more than I loved her; now I know how
she felt.

22 April.
This day made a Last Will & Testament leaving Fanny
everything, save the Still, which goes to Lambright & Coffinberry for being my witnesses & executors.

23 April.
Today gave Lettiece permission to live with us if she
swears off booze.
"I already has, Massa."
Fanny melancholy; she feels sinful about becoming betrothed so soon after Henry's death. Before I could reply,
we were joined in her cabin by Mrs. Cooper & Beam, at
whose insistence the Rev. has gone to condemn Stump for
adultery.

24 April.
Split & stripped saplings in the rain all day.

25 April. Sun. eve.
With Fanny after Meeting in Central Park. Told her I'm adding a snug wattle & daub room to the front of my cabin.

A sudden shower drove us into Williams' Tavern. Fanny said, "Ma hates Carrie—not just 'cause she's a girl. Carrie makes her feel old."

The rain let up some. She said, "Thank God for Pa! Poor Pa! He didn't have no luck with Billy or Martha. Billy told him, 'I don't believe there's a Hell.' "

28 April.
Bought this morn. of Jones at his store, Mans.,
1 lb. wrought nails.. .14.
Sold to the above, 8 gall. whisky, 80 proof, @
.32... $2.56.

Which he waters & swaps for peltry with the Delaware. Eight drunken bucks & squaws on Park Ave., including the old woman who threw herself on the corpse.

29 April.
Took off work on roof today to discover how the owls are faring. Nest deserted, obviously for some time. Pru barked at the month-old birds huddled together under a scrub oak. Great fluffy balls. They had eaten a black duck, of which only the bill, a few bones & feathers remained.

Even Mrs. Cooper smiles at Pru, who vanishes for hours immediately the Rev. takes his sawed-off rifle down from the wall.

"She's a cheerful coward," says Fanny.

Sarah calls her "Pruzie"; as does the Rev.

All are slightly scared of her. (Lettiece is terrified.) The dog has twice snatched a 5 lb. cheese from the table & devoured it on the spot. Fanny explained,

"She looks at you sideways, head down, the cheese 'twixt

her jaws, and when you reach for it, she growls. At the same time, she wags her tail. Which end should you trust? You hesitate; the cheese is lost. Gobbled up. Such a smart dog!"

Fanny will still be nursing after we're married. Her stained bodice, its smell, excites & disgusts me.

30 April. 11 PM.
Chapman here.
3 AM.
> *Lines on My Talk Tonight with C.*

> There are moments
> When, like he,
> I know the Earth
> To be alive,
> But disagree that
> She can know the same—
> Or anything—
> Of me.

1 May.
I have in ready money .... $26.515.
Received in full this morn. from the Rev., ½ his
monthly profit from the sale of dairy produce....   .415.

He and I forgave Chapman for stirring up Tommy Lyons.
C.: "I'll never forgive myself. I was bamboozled by Self-Love. I believed God was working a miracle—Tommy Lyons' Vision—thro' me."
He left with the Rev. about 1 PM to beg forgiveness of Mrs. Cooper & Fanny.

2 May.
Paid in full to Jacob Beam for cracking 350 lbs.
my corn, for which I sold him 1 gall., 3 gills,
whisky, 80 proof..   .35.
                                                                 .35.

Frost; cold rainy day.

3 May.
Off the booze two months today.
Another rainy Sun. morn, in Mans., with Fanny. She spoke about her Father dying of the diabetes at 42 yrs. of age—how his strength failed, appetite decayed & flesh wasted away. Said she,
"He was skin and bones, save his feet. They swelled. Like Henry's."
I am a year older than her Father when he died.
Chapman's whereabouts are unknown.

5 May.
Grubbed out the old turnip bed.

6 May.
Saw a number of beaver & some otter today; killed 2 of the former, also a doe.

7 May.
Strawberry bed cleaned out. My poor back!

8 May.
A run of 14 gall. whisky, 80 proof.

9 May.
Chapman's news from Greentown:
1. Backed by about 60 warriors, Armstrong's word—"We-lung-goon-doon!"—"Peace!"—is Law.
2. A young buck named Fling-Her-This-Way paid Tommy Lyons a large clasp knife to put a curse on the girl who spurned him. After she suffered 4 fainting fits in as many days, her father paid Tommy Lyons 10 lbs. of pig tail tobacco to remove same, which he did.
3. The drunken old squaw whose son was killed by the arrow hanged herself in her cabin.

C. said, "I forgive myself everything. I must, or play the sinner even more than I do. Lord, I love playing the sinner!"

10 May.

Sold to Jones, at his store, Mans., 2 beaver skins ... $4.00.
Sold to the above, 5 gall. whisky, 80 proof .... 1.60.
Bought of the above, 1 razor .... .08.
Bought " ", ¼ lb. cinnamon .... .20.

The third rainy Sun. in a row.

According to "The Chill. Ind. Rep.," Ohio mustered 30,000 militiamen, from which Gov. Meigs picked 1200 of the best who are presently quartered in Dayton; they will join Hull & his Michigan volunteers invading Upper Canada, via Detroit, immediately war is declared.

Beam, who's familiar with those parts, predicts a tough campaign—very tough, even in summer.

Fanny said of him, "He's a good godfather. You don't take enough heed of Carrie."

13 May.

Kidney beans & cabbages out.

14 May.

Ditto, pease & lima beans.

15 May.

An Ohio saying: "When the oak's leaf is the size of a mouse's ear, hunt sponge mushrooms." Found a bushel of them (*Morchella esculenta* L.) under the elms cross the creek today.

17 May.

A sunny Sun. spent mostly abed, staring at the ceiling, knees raised—my only comfortable position since I finished planting potatoes yesterday afternoon.

Mrs. Lambright knows I'm betrothed! Back to bed.

19 May.

Sat up this morn., feet upon the floor, & lo, my back snapped into place. I screamed. Mrs. Lambright said,

"Take it easy for another day or two."

She has been sleeping these last 2 nights wrapped up in a blanket on the new room's earthen floor.

She swore to keep my betrothal secret & said,

"Fanny was worried you didn't come to town and asked us to look in on you."

"Truly?"

"She cares about you."

Coffinberry persuaded old man Seymour, our Orderly Sergeant, to call a General Muster in Central Park after Meeting next week. Seymour's mind wanders; we must elect another in his stead. Will nominate Lambright, who entered our Country's service as a militiaman in N.J. on 30 Sept., 1776—his 19th birthday—& fought 5 yrs.

20 May.

No pain. After putting out my onions & leeks, Mrs. Lambright accepted the bushel of dried mushrooms as a token of my gratitude & returned home.

Sleet (7:10 PM).

21 May.

Cold rain till afternoon.

22 May.

Paid in full to Jacob Beam at his mill, for
cracking 300 lbs. my corn, for which I sold him
1 gall. less 2 gills, whisky, 80 proof .... .30.
                                                                .30.

The Rev. has given him "The Causes, Evils & Cures of Church & Heart Divisions." Beam studies it an hour a day.

"I got great responsibilities as Carrie's godfather."

This day marks the 32nd Anniversary of Mother's death.

23 May.

Fair weather continues. Have decided upon a puncheon floor for the new room. Split and hewed logs—red oak—all day without ill effect to my back.

24 May.

Sold this morn. to Jones, at his store, Mans., 5
gall. whisky, 80 proof... $1.60.
Bought of the above, 1 lb. bar lead.................... 1.00.
Bought ½ lb. rifle powder............................... .50.

Lambright elected Orderly Sergeant over Bob Coffinberry by a vote of 7–5. Chapman abstained; he never bears arms. Bob remains our Drum Major. Beam will teach Sam Lewis Jr. to play his fife.

Henceforth, save Chapman, we will assemble every Sunday at 3 PM in Central Park equipped with:

rifle or musket
2 hickory or one steel or iron ram rod & extra spring
    worm
priming wire & brush
at least 15 bullets or rounds of cartridges
6 flints
tow for wadding
one lb. powder
butcher knife
hatchet or tomahawk
knapsack & blanket
canteen or wood bottle to hold 1 qt.

Shared with Fanny my memories of Mother's death:
"She was out of her head the last three days, shouting things like, 'An apron! Green baize!' Pa was with the Army in Morristown, New Jersey. His brother, Uncle Joe, who was Pastor at Holden and a widower—the man who raised me after Pa died—he called to me in the yard when she lost consciousness.

"I squeezed her hand, knowing she couldn't see or hear me.

"She died five hours later that night at twenty one minutes past ten.

"I was 11 years old."

Carrie smiles at Fanny & reaches for her.

25 May.

Have dragged down & lined off my fields. Covered over garden with cedar boughs.

26 May.

Just in time! Frost this morn. & now (noon) hail.

27 May.

Another memory: Mother's death-rattle, half-opened eyes.

28 May.

Killed a rabbit in the pease.

29 May.

Made 30 bullets.

30 May.

This day's run of 12 gall. whisky, 80 proof, from my Still makes me crave a drink more than usual.

Haven't forgot how to throw the tomahawk.

31 May.

Sold to Jones, at his store, Mans., 5 gall. whisky, 80 proof .... $1.60.

Bob Coffinberry played a long roll upon his snare drum, then Lambright shouted,

"Position of the soldier at my order: Arms! Take heed, Phil! Billy, eyes front! Watch me! (louder) Arms!!! See? The heel of the butt is on a line with the little toe of my right foot. My right hand holds the piece near the muzzle—so!"

The upright piece is brought with the right hand to the center of the body, ram rod in front. Left hand at the same time supports the whole weight by grasping stock; little finger touching featherspring, thumb up, elbow in. The thumb of the right hand placed in the rear of the small of the stock steadies the piece.

Noon. With Fanny at Williams' tending C. He has been sleeping in the shallow limestone cave on the Rocky Fork & suffers from congested lungs. She took him home.

1 June.

I have in ready money	$32.95.
Received here in full from the Rev. Cooper, ½ his monthly profit from the sale of dairy produce	.27.

The womenfolk take turns blistering C., who has a high fever.

The Rev. believes the impending war is unjust & impolitic—inflicted upon us by the atheistical Jefferson; his embargo, etc. etc.

I said, "The prospect excites me."

4 June.

Have hilled & planted the seed corn acquired from Coffinberry—a species made by Man!

5 June.

Cloudy with drippings all afternoon. Put in cucumbers.

6 June.

Ditto, pumpkins & squash. A sore back.

7 June. Sun.

Skipped muster. Went instead to discover if Chapman was still at the Coopers'. His illness has aged him 5 years. On the other hand, all spruced up, he is comely.

He said, "Beth spoke to me Monday morning. She'd no news of Henry."

Fanny (later): "Tom, I don't care about Henry no more. Our talk made me realize how much I miss my father. And yearn to be with him. That's Heaven to me—Eternal Bliss; being with Pa."

13 June.

Carrie was 5 months old today. I offered my felicitations to Fanny, who was much pleased. She & Chapman argued at supper about Swedenborg's Heavenly Doctrine. She said,

"No, I can't accept it. I'll die a Methodist. My father-in-law's Easter Sermon brung me back to the fold."

"Yes," said I. "It was very beautiful."

"Have you then come back to Christ?"

"We do not share the same beliefs, but that is a matter best discussed by us in private."

"You are right," she said, lowering her eyes.

14 June.

Sold to Jones at his store, Mans., 5 gall. whisky,
80 proof .... $1.60.

Neither Phil nor Stump at muster.

"They can't stand being in the same place at the same time," says Lambright.

He repeated last Sun.'s lesson: "Present Arms!" Afterwards, I praised Fanny for her decision re Swedenborg. This time, looking me in the eye, she replied,

"I must say I hold with one of his notions: the love of dominion, one over the other, entirely takes away marital delights."

15 June. 10:30 PM.
Masturbatus sum. (Juvenal).

16 June. 11 AM.
Drunk.

18 June. 11 AM.
Juvenal.

19 June.
Constipated since Tues. Took a strong purge: ragweed root. (*Ambrosia artemisiifolia* L.)

20 June. 3 PM.
Juvenal.

23 June.
Spent Sun. & Mon. mostly abed. Fanny hither this morn. for the first time.
"Tom, you must repent! I cannot marry an infidel. It breaks my heart."

25 June.
Crows in the corn.

26 June.
Lettiece here this morn. to wash clothes. We split a pint of booze, fucked. "Thank you, Massa!"
Black, wiry hair on her twat, which is pink.
She was excited by the smell of my feet. Ditto, sounds of sucking, lapping. Doesn't like ears licked.
Chief Armstrong fucked her only in the dark. Kept his leggins and moccasons on. "In and out."
Del. word for fuck: Au-hole-to-wok-con.
For pecker: Lin-no-wa-la-ka-ka-pis.
For twat: Naid-lah-done-rom-na-pat-ter. (Hairy mouth without teeth!)

27 June. 10 AM.
Drunk.

28 June. Sun.
Sold to Jones, at his store, Mans., 2 gall. whisky,
80 proof .... .64.

Col. William ("Dutch") Kratzer of the Mt. Vernon Rifles addressed us in Central Park: "Gallant Sons of Ohio! By an act of Congress passed on the 18th of this month, our Country is at war! Kill the British and their savage hirelings! Canada is ours! I'm drunk!"

He puked. Lambright was promoted Capt. by unanimous acclamation. The Rev. exhorted everyone over 7 years old to observe Wed. (1 July) as a Day of Fasting & Prayer. Beam: "Amen!"

Tommy Lyons watched.

1 July.

I have in ready money .... $35.36.

In the year since I began this Waste Book, I have doubled my cash!

2 July.

Paid to Jacob Beam, for cracking 330 lbs. my
corn.. .33.
Received here in full from the Rev. Cooper, ½
of his profit from the sale of dairy produce........ .21.

About the war: "God's will be done!"

About Fanny: "God be praised! I have not lived in vain! She says she has returned to the true faith because of my Easter Sermon!"

About Lettiece: "Dutiful, obedient; she is the perfect servant!"

3 July.

Repaired fireplace.

4 July.   Sat.

Bought of Jones, at his store, Mans., 4 sticks,
India ink, @ .11 .... .44.
Bought of the above, 3 steel pens, @ .01 .... .03.
Bought 1 linen girth .... .60.

Chapman read the Declaration of Independence & the Rev. said a short prayer. Sam Lewis Jr. & Bob Coffinberry played "Free America" & "Yankee Doodle" upon the fife & drum. Mrs. Lambright unfurled a 3½′ × 5′ silken flag sewn by our womenfolk. Still only 15 stars. None yet for Tennessee (1796), Ohio (1803), or our youngest sister, Louisiana, admitted to the Union, 30 April, this year.

"Present Arms!"

"The Chillicothe Independent Republican" has become "The Fredonian"; it reports Gen. Hull's army of Ohio Volunteers will reach Detroit about 10 July. The subjugation of the nearby British post of Fort Malden—notorious for sheltering hostile Indians—is expected next. "We think it highly probable that this will be the first event of the war that we shall have the pleasure to announce."

5 July.

There being no muster today, I ran 12½ gall. whisky, 80 proof.

6 July.

This afternoon in exchange for ½ pt. (watered) booze, Lettiece allowed me to lick her ears, which makes her shudder. We fucked behind the barn. "Thank you, Massa!"

7 July.

Repaired chimney.

11 July. 9:30 AM.

Drunk.

12 July.

Sold to Jones at his store, Mans., 3 gall. whisky, 80 proof..	.96.
Sold to Billy Stump, the use of 3 balls & my M 1803, exclusive of powder, to shoot at the mark in Central Park...	.10.

He won first prize—a calico shirt. Phil too drunk to compete.

Tommy Lyons watched.

From "The Fredonian": The U.S. ship of war "Oneida" has been captured & sent into Kingston by the British on Lake Ontario.

13 July.

Carrie 6 months old today. Smiles at the sound of her mother's voice. Fanny complained that Mrs. Cooper gives her a hard time. "Marry me, Tom!"

"But I am an infidel."

"I forgive you. Marry me!"

"I will think about it."

"Don't you love me no more?"

"You know I do."

"Then marry me."

"I will think about it."

Supped with Mrs. Cooper & the Rev. He spoke about his failure to convert any Del. Part of the trouble is the poverty of their language. The Lord's Prayer must be boiled down to:

"Our Father, hallowed (a-ha-le-mok-hock-ek) be Thy name. Forgive us as we forgive. Deliver us. For Thine is the kingdom (lea-kock). Amen."

11:30 PM. Rain.

Fanny will never forgive me for getting back at her. I saw it in her eyes.

16 July.

Picked my first bushel of apples, which are very large, greenish-yellow, crisp & sweet.

17 July.

Henry Cooper died a year ago today. Offered condolences at noon. Grasped Fanny's hands. The Rev., short of cash, asked me to accept butter &/or cheese in payment for Juno on the 1st. Inst. I agreed.

18 July.

Behind the barn this afternoon, in exchange for 1 pint of (watered) booze, Lettiece said,

"I was cried off to Massa Sloat for three hundred dollars in the Lewisburg livery stable that Monday morning. Massa Hammond—a white beaver pushed back on his head—he stripped me naked and said, 'Up on the stool, gal! Stand straight! Make your mammy proud!'

"A gentleman wearing a plaid vest, he say, 'Bend over,' to me, and looks for worms. Like this. (Raising her skirt above her hips.) Stick your finger up. Go on. Now wriggle it. Not so hard! Not so hard! (Turning around & pulling off her dress.) Tickle my titties with your tongue. Ah!"

Then we fucked. "Thank you, Massa!"

11 PM. Drunk.

18 July.

Paid to Jacob Beam for cracking 350 lbs. my
corn... .35.

10 PM. Drunk.

19 July.

Sold to Jones, at his store, Mans., 3 gall. whisky,
80 proof .... .96.

Made Chapman a gift of 1 doz. apples, which he identified as "American Gloria Mundi."

From "The Fredonian": "We are happy to announce the glorious news that Gen. Hull & his army have landed safely in Canada and taken possession of the town of Sandwich, two miles below Detroit on the British side. On to Fort Malden! Glory! Glory! to the Ohio volunteers!"

Fanny embraced Lettiece on Diamond St., crying, "Now you must stay with me always!"

"Oh, I will Missy. I will!"

The Rev. explained, "Lettiece hoped to live in Canada."

20 July.

Chapman here at sunup. We breakfasted on apple sauce.

He said, "I ain't heard from Beth in over eight months. How I miss her!"

A run of 13 gall. whisky, 80 proof.

25 July.

Off the booze three days; the shakes, insomnia till last night, when I slept 12 hours.

8 PM. A 4 hour nap this afternoon.

26 July.

Sold to Jones, at his store, Mans., 5 gall. whisky, 80 proof .... $1.60.

While I was there, Tommy Lyons & his mute Mingo slave swapped 8 bear skins for 14 common gunlocks—Jones' entire stock.

From "The Fredonian": "We have been informed that Tecumseh sent out an Indian from Fort Malden, in the forepart of last week, with a wampum belt 3 feet wide & 6 feet long (painted red as an emblem of war) to rouse all Indians on the N.W. frontier."

31 July. 7:30 PM.

10th day without a drink.

1 August.

I have in ready money .... $38.94.

Received here in full from the Rev. Cooper, 12¼ lbs. cheese.

Fanny & Mrs. Cooper haven't spoken to each other in over a month.

Carrie has a chest cold.

2 August. Sun. 5 PM.

Chopped wood for Still. Rain since noon.

3 August.

While Carrie had a cold, she learned to cough; tho' fully recovered, she coughed all morn. with obvious delight.

Fanny & I gossiped about Phil, Martha & Billy. Fanny: "The ones I worry about are Billy's poor wife and kids."

Lettiece on old man Seymour: "You know what they say— 'Once grown and twice a chile.' "

4 August. Wed.

Sold to Jones, at his store, Mans., 5 gall. whisky,
80 proof... $1.60.
Sold to Williams, at his tavern, 6 lbs. cheese, for
which he owes to pay me on the 16th Inst. .... .60.

Armstrong's son Silas drunk at the bar.

8 August.

Paid to Lettiece Shipman, behind my barn
earlier this eve., for which she again allowed me
to be the gentleman in the plaid vest .... .35.

plus 1 pt. watered booze.

"Strip naked!"
"Yes, Massa!"
"Now undress me. First my boots."
"Yes, Massa!"
"Grab your knees! Do as you're told. Bend over, gal!"
"Yes, Massa!"
"This is my forefinger. Does it hurt?"
"No, Massa."

"That?"

"Yes, Massa!"

"Does this?"

"Yes, Massa!"

"Now, on your back!"

"Yes, Massa."

"Spread your legs wider!"

"You got no steel in your barrel!"

"Stand up!"

"Yes, Massa."

"Straighten up, shoulders back, stick out your titties. Make your Mammy proud! Nice. Any worms, gal?"

"No, Massa."

"Turn around. Bend over. Spread your cheeks!"

"Yes, Massa."

"Does that hurt?"

"Yes, Massa!"

"Now, quick. Down on your knees. Open your mouth! Suck! That's it! That's it! Now, say it!"

"Thank you, Massa."

11 PM. *Masturbatus sum.* (Lettiece).

9 August.

Sold to Jones, at his store, Mans., 2 gall. whisky,
80 proof .... .64.

From "The Fredonian":

On Saturday, the 1st. Inst., the family of a Mr. Mix, living on Little Pigeon Creek, near the Ohio River, in Indiana Territory, were attacked by three Indians about day light—old Mrs. Mix was first fired on as she was going to the spring, but sustained no injury. Her husband, who ran into the yard, was shot dead. Her youngest son was shot in the knee and his arm broke by tomahawks. Another son, who lived close by, heard the screams, ran over, and shot one of the Indians in the head. He got the old lady and the wounded man into the house and beat off the two remaining Indians.

Lambright announced at muster that if there's trouble here, "Dutch" Kratzer has promised us the Mt. Vernon Rifles—35 mounted militiamen.
Chapman: "I'll fetch 'em!"
The Rev. volunteered his mare, Liz.
Tommy Lyons watched.

11 August.
Paid in full to Jacob Beam for cracking 320 lbs. my corn, for which I gave him 1 gall. whisky,
80 proof .... .32.
.32.

12 August.
Dog Days end. Dry.

14 August.
Killed a fawn late this afternoon.

15 August.
A run of 12 gall. whisky, 80 proof.
25th day without a drink.

16 August.
Sold to Jones, at his store, Mans., 5 gall. whisky,
80 proof .... $1.60.

Lambright drunk at muster. Today is the 4th anniversary of the death of his 7 yr. old daughter, Hazel, from the cholera in Pittsburgh.
"The Fredonian": "Gen. Hull, after entering Canada, wrote to the Secretary of War in Washington City that he was strong enough in arms, ammunition, guns, gun-carriages

& provisions to subdue Fort Malden. Within four miles of his goal, Hull ordered the army back to Detroit. We demand to know why!"

20 August.   9 AM.
Jones hither from Mans. with news brought there by a dispatch rider from Warren to Pittsburgh: Detroit is lost! Hull & his army surrendered Sun., 16 Aug. 9 boats laden with 300 British regulars & 600 Indians have landed on the S. shore of Lake Erie near the mouth of the Huron river about 50 miles NE of here.

Jones: "This man got his information from the Cleveland express rider to Warren named Zach Moorman. I know Zach Moorman. I trust him. Spread the word south along the Black Fork. Everybody come quick to Central Park!"

3:30 PM.   Central Park. Lambright drunk. Today is the 4th anniversary of the death of his 5 yr. old daughter, Hannah, from the cholera in Pitts.

Drum Major Beam has taken temporary command. We will build a blockhouse atop the rise behind his mill. Martha weeps. Billy showed her the following to his wife in Cincinnati:

My dearest Em & Boys,
    If I live thro' this trouble, I will fetch you here. That I swear!
    Yours truly,
                                      (Sgd.) William Stump.

4 PM.   The Rev. off to assure Armstrong of our desire for peace. Chapman has gone N. to warn folks in the Huron Valley about the British & Indians.

My biggest worry—Fanny. And Carrie!!! She has her father's comely hands, and dark hair. Fanny's blue eyes. She will never be as pretty as her mother.

21 August. 5:30 AM.
  Beam's mill.

The felling party:	The raising party:
Billy	Me
Lambright	Phil
Sam Lewis	Bob Coffinberry
" " Jr.	Jones
Geo. Coffinberry	The Rev. (when he
Williams	returns)

Beam, who once served as a Pioneer at Fort Deposit under
Gen. Wayne, is in charge of construction of the blockhouse.
Sides are to be laid horizontally & halved together at the
ends like a log cabin. We will also dig a well and erect an 8
foot high stockade, its gate facing the creek.
  10 AM. The Rev. has returned, declaring, "We won't
have no trouble with the Delaware at Greentown. Chief
Armstrong gave me his word."
  Phil said, "Well, I don't trust him."
  "You're wrong!"
  9 PM. Carried logs with the Rev. for the stockade all
afternoon. Rubbed our shoulders raw. Fanny applied a cool
poultice of boiled pine bark. She has fine reddish-gold hairs
on her forearms.

22 August.
  One month without a drink.
  From Thursday's "Fredonian":

DETROIT IS TAKEN!!!

  Capt. Wm. Keys of the first company of Chillicothe
volunteers, has just arrived in town from Detroit, and
confirms the intelligence that Hull has shamefully, inglo-

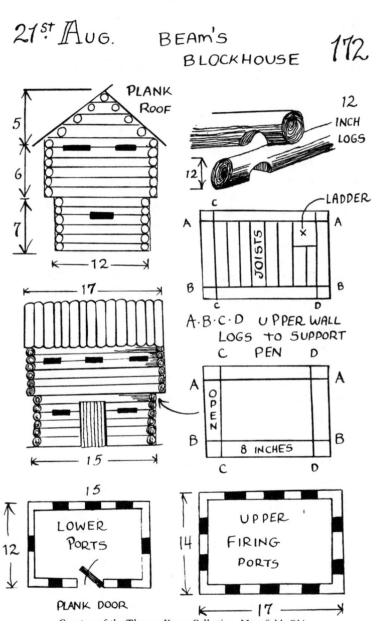

21ˢᵗ Aᵤɢ.   BEAM'S BLOCKHOUSE   112

PLANK ROOF

12 INCH LOGS

5
6
7
12

17
15

LADDER
C
A   A
JOISTS   ×
B   B
C   D

A·B·C·D UPPER WALL
LOGS to SUPPORT
PEN
C   D
A   A
OPEN
B   B
8 INCHES
C   D

15
LOWER PORTS
12
PLANK DOOR

UPPER FIRING PORTS
14
17

Courtesy of the Thomas Keene Collection, Mansfield, Ohio.

riously and disgracefully surrendered to the British and Indians. Our brave Volunteers and the Heroes of Tippecanoe are prisoners of War. Three or four days previous to the base surrender of Detroit, while the British were erecting batteries, Hull would not permit a gun to be fired at them. Our riflemen could have picked them off like pigeons.

About 1500 British and Indians crossed the Detroit River in broad day light, under a flag of truce. Hull capitulated, without resistance. The gates of the fort were opened, and our brave soldiers piled their arms before an inferior force.

Eternal infamy must cover Hull! He has let loose thousands of merciless savages on our defenseless frontiers—the blood of many hundred helpless women and children must rest on his head.

Well, we have lost an army. But Britain and her savage allies shall see that we are descendants of heroes. We backwoodsmen are roused. Let our enemies beware!

We have time to add only that the regulars were taken in captivity to Quebec. The Volunteers were sent home. Col. McArthur's reg't. will be here in a few days.

23 August.   Sun.
Sold to Luther Coe, 2 gall. whisky,
     80 proof .... $1.28.
  "   " Alvin Coe, 1 gall. whisky,
     80 proof .... .64.
  "   " Caleb Palmer, 1 gall. whisky,
     80 proof .... .64.
  "   " (?) McIntyre, 1 qt. whisky,
     80 proof .... .16.
  "   " Erastus Smith, 1 pt. whisky,
     80 proof .... .08.

The above, with their families, teams, cattle, etc., arrived

Mans. at 10 AM after a 10 hr. trip in the rain from New Haven on the Upper Huron. They swam the swelled river below Plymouth, led by Caleb Palmer.

Tall, fat, 51 years of age; wears spectacles. As he was rounding up his cows in the woods late Fri. afternoon, he heard a cry:

"Run for your life! The British and Indians have landed at Huron!"

It was Chapman, whose tatters, pasteboard visor & bare feet bemuse Palmer. He can't understand why Thurs. "Fredonian" (see above) doesn't mention landings. A false alarm? Intends to verify tomorrow in Mt. Vernon. Meanwhile, has pitched camp with the others in Central Park.

None of them know Chapman's whereabouts now. He was last seen by Erastus Smith & his pretty wife on Fri. eve. Mrs. Smith—Ellen—exhausted, feverish, chilled from her 27 mile journey atop a swaying, squealing cart. Ditto, Mrs. Palmer, whose 5 yr. old son, Joab, has a sore throat.

25 August.
    Bought of Jones, at his store, Mans., 1 shoe
    knife .... .16.
    Bought 1 shoe nipper .... .30.

New Haven folks heading home. Palmer: "That lunatick Chapman spread a false alarm."

He breakfasted yesterday with "Dutch" Kratzer at Slocum's Tavern, Mt. Vernon. An express rider from Cleveland arrived about noon. Capt. Aaron Huffman, commanding the militia there, wrote Kratzer in a letter,

"My scouts assure me that no British soldiers or savages have landed on the S. shore (of Lake Erie)."

3 PM. Rain. Asked Fanny to marry me. "Oh, Tom! Yes!" War excites us. Kissed her lips; she opened her mouth. Lettiece at the flax wheel gave me a look. Will have both.

26 August.

The Rev. has agreed to marry us.

He said, "Promise me two things. Bring Carrie up in the true faith and stay off the booze."

"Carrie will be my daughter to be raised as I see fit. But you have my word I will never take another drink."

"Fair enough."

27 August.

Phil spied out Greentown early this morn. "A squaw named Lo-kas-kway—Bowl Woman—gave birth to a boy with white skin and reddish-brown hair. Some of them little bastards are born that way, then turn dark.

"Armstrong keeps to his cabin. Tommy Lyons is hunting up the Rocky Fork."

28 August.

Chapman: "Congratulations! I hope you and Fanny will be happy! You must wish me the same. Beth spoke to me the night I left the Smith place. She said, 'Johnny, you're to be allowed two wives in Heaven! Me and Peggy Owens. She's 13 years old, a New York City girl, who fell down a well and drownded on December 9, 1765.' "

"My best wishes to you both."

"All three of us."

"All three of you."

31 August. Sun. Noon.

Beam's blockhouse.

Yesterday, about 3 PM, outside his store on the corner of Main & Park Ave. W., Levi Jones was stabbed in the throat and scalped by Mahk-wa-tut—Little Bear—the 12 year old boy who sang at last winter's Vision Ceremony.

Williams: "I was sweeping up behind the bar, when I heard the scalp Halloo. By the time I made it to the door with my rifle, Little Bear and 5 or 6 other Del. bucks, all painted red and black, were mounted up. Little Bear yelled, 'Hoo! Hoo! Hoo!' and waved Jones' bloody scalp. I know him from way back; a quiet kid. All arms and legs. He traded peltry with Jones.''

Williams got off one shot at Little Bear, but missed. The bucks rode N.

At the funeral here this morn., the Rev. took as his text, Jer. 48:10, "Cursed be he who doeth the work of the Lord deceitfully; & cursed be he who keepeth back his sword from blood.''

1 PM. Chapman back from Mt. Vernon with "Dutch" Kratzer, Capt. Reed Douglas, & 40 mounted militiamen, 4th Reg. 4th Brigade, 2nd Div. Ohio Militia.

3 PM. Bob Coffinberry & 15 volunteers from the Mt. Vernon Rifles—Capt. Douglas commanding—have started on Little Bear's trail.

11 PM. Williams tells me that Jones came from Shenandoah Co., Va., & settled in Pleasant Township, Fairfield Co., Ohio, in 1807 with his mother, Clara Thomas, and stepbrother Michael. Jones returned to Va. for a yr. before settling in Mans., April, 1809. He was 38 yrs. old.

1 Sept.
Beam's blockhouse.

I have in ready money	$44.20.
Received here in full from the Rev. Cooper, ½ his monthly profit from the sale of dairy produce	.08.

Kratzer, who supped with us, is also building a blockhouse— in Central Park. A left-handed, blue-eyed Dutchman, 62, b. in Hesse-Hanau. He emigrated at 7 yrs. of age to Philadelphia with his gunsmith father. Married Eliza Wolfe of Lehigh

County, Pa. No kids. Settled on a quarter section, Owl Creek, Ashland County, 1805. They own Slocum's Tavern, both whore houses, the brickyard in Mt. Vernon.

Martha weeps all the time. Now that Billy's wife will join him, he & Phil have become pals.

Mrs. Cooper couldn't be nicer to me—& Fanny!—since we announced our betrothment.

7 PM.   Carrie's red, swelled fingers, ears, toes—fleas.

Lambright has posted the following daily work roster:

Scout	John Chapman
Hunting	John Lambright, Phil Seymour, Sam Lewis, Isaac Williams
Tend stock, gather firewood, draw water	Thom. Keene, Rev. Cooper, Sam Lewis, Jr.
Mill	Jacob & Katherine ("Ma") Beam
Laundry	Grace Lewis, Hattie Lambright, Lettiece
Privy	Lettiece
Cooking	Clarissa Cooper, Martha Seymour, Delight Coffinberry, "Ma" Beam
Tending children	Fanny Cooper, Sarah Cooper, Lettiece

Geo., Sam & Billy are detailed to weed & hoe everyone's corn, gather vegetables & check Williams' Tavern, Bob's forge, Jones' store.

Guard Duty

The 12 of us are divided into teams of 2 men. (Am with the Rev.) Each team serves 4 hrs. We rotate every other day so that no one gets stuck with night duty all the time.

2 Sept.
Beam's blockhouse.
7 PM. Pulled fodder all day. A sore back.
Central Park blockhouse & stockade finished. Kratzer also informs us that this afternoon he received orders, via dispatch rider, from Gen. Harrison, at his headquarters, Lower Piqua, to remove the Del. of Greentown there.
11 PM. We men sleep on the ground floor. Me between Lambright & the Rev.; old man Seymour by the door because of his weak bladder. Women and children upstairs.

3 Sept.
Beam's blockhouse.
Jethro Stone, Kratzer's scout, hither from the latter at Central Park blockhouse. Kratzer will arrive here about 5 AM with 23 mounted riflemen, his plan to remove Del. from Greentown.

Stone, on Kratzer's capacity as officer, "Good as a nigger, anytime."

Stone has been fighting Indians hereabouts since 27 May, 1794, when he & 16 Virginians from Fort Baker ambushed a Del. war party under Chief Pipe at Captina Creek.

"Our first volley killed 3 and wounded 5, one mortally. The others formed a hollow square, faced out behind the trees, and beat us off.

"Delaware warriors, like all Indians, obey their officers immediately. And without being flogged! They're disciplined.

"Indians handle weapons very well. They fight light—no canteens, knapsacks, blankets, compasses, cartridge cases. They fight naked save breech-clouts, leggins and moccasons, in all kinds of weather. They thrive on a couple of mouthfuls of parched corn and a drink of water twice a day. Why, they train up their boys to the art of war since the age of 12.

"We mustn't be too proud to learn from them. We ain't above borrowing their words—hommony, pone, moccason, tomahawk. I tell you, if we fight like Indians, what with our

Beam's Blockhouse
Second Story

matress   Carrie

me
(Sarah Cooper).   Fanny

Ma

by
Sarah Elizabeth Cooper

Courtesy of the Thomas Keene Collection, Mansfield, Ohio.

mechanical genius, no European power would dare set foot in the American woods."

4 Sept.

Beam's blockhouse.

4 AM. Lambright & Chapman, who spied out Greentown about 2 hrs. ago, heard drums, "The Rattlesnake Song," from the Council House. ("Rattlesnake/rattlesnake/Give us your power/all winter long!")

Tommy Lyons, Little Bear & a score of other warriors haven't been home in over 10 days, says Little Bear's Ma, whom C. bribed with a peck of salt.

Lambright: "Chief Armstrong still commands 41 fighting men. 15 more than us!"

5:30 AM. Kratzer vs. the Rev., who says that the Del. remaining in Greentown are innocent of Jones' murder. Removing them from their homes, hunting grounds, ancestral graves a terrible crime. "God will punish us!"

"My orders, sir, are to remove them, and however unjust it might be, I can do no less than obey orders."

The Rev. finally said, "If I can't stop you, I must at least try and prevent bloodshed. Let me powwow with Armstrong. I'll guarantee him the lives and property of his people if he surrenders."

Kratzer: "Suit yourself."

6:15 AM. We have unanimously adopted Lambright's plan:

"Except Johnny, the Rev. and Col. Kratzer, we'll be mounted. There's 33 of us. They have but 7 horsemen, including Armstrong.

"Spread out with your backs to the east wall of the Council House, on either side of me. You'll be facing about 125 Delaware, with the sun in their eyes, listening to the Rev. and the Col. palaver with Armstrong. Pay them no mind!

"Look in the crowd for bucks with guns! Find the one nearest you on horseback, then the nearest one afoot. If—

and only if—I blow two short blasts on my hunting horn—
like this—shoot your man on horseback, then ride the other
down and tomahawk him. Any one of them is twice the man
you are, but in that crowd, he'll be worried about his wife
and kids. That's our real advantage. Now clean and load
your pieces."

Phil: "Hands off Armstrong. He's mine!"

The Rev. asked me to remain at his side & record what
happens. Lambright will cover me. Have agreed; being
unarmed will bring me luck. Feel it in my bones.

8 AM.   Have left $, paintings, with Fanny. Lambright will
burn this book if I am blinded (my great fear) or killed.

11 AM.   Armstrong replied to the Rev., saying, in effect,
"Kan-ot-chy (Tommy Lyons) was a drunkard. He was a
disgrace to his father, the Wolf clan, & his nation. He was
ah-lux-soo (empty, without a Guardian Spirit).

"Then En-naughk, My Father (Chapman), with the help
of Jesus Christ got him our Mother, the Earth, Ka-ha-suna
herself! She commanded him,

" 'Join Tecumseh & his brother, The Shawanoe Prophet.
Protect me! I suffer terrible pain when a white man cuts my
breast with his plough,' Ka-ha-suna told him. 'Kill them all.' "

He said the men, women & children under our guns are
innocent of Jones' murder.

The Rev. guaranteed that we will protect and preserve
Del. lives & property. C. then translated Kratzer:

"You will be removed to Mans., where you must answer
roll call every evening. Any Indian caught in the woods will
be shot. From there, you will be marched to the Johnson
farm in Upper Piqua, & given suitable provisions till war's
end. The American government will also provide you with
a blacksmith. You will be allowed to return here—with said
blacksmith—after the war."

Armstrong: "We will surrender all our guns and weapons
of war, answering to roll call every day! But here we stay!"

"No, sir! I must take you away!"

"We will not fight—but only because of our women and children!" In English: "Fuck you! Fuck America!" To C. & the Rev. on his right: "Fuck Jesus Christ!"

Kratzer: "You may keep your pipe tomahawks, scalpers, bows and arrows."

1 PM. They surrendered 38 muskets, 4 rifles, 123 lbs. lead, 46 lbs. powder, 2 (rusty) Ames sabres, 41 tomahawks, 25 lbs. swan shot, 123 flints & one set of gunsmith's tools.

Then they took away the fences round the graves, leveled & covered them with green sod.

5 Sept. 7 AM.
Beam's blockhouse.

Lambright & Jethro Stone made a list of Del. property, & about 5 PM, we took up our line of march across the Black Fork toward the new state road. There we saw smoke above the treetops behind us. Phil & 8 militiamen, who stayed in Greentown, burned it down. Nearly everything was consumed—43 log cabins, the Council House & much personal property which the Del. were unable to carry with them. They are encamped under guard in the ravine, Mans.

6 Sept. 6 PM. Sun.
Beam's blockhouse.

The Rev's morn. sermon:

"From 'The Song of Deborah,' Judges, Chapter 5, Verses 24–27. 'Blessed above women shall Jael the wife of Heber the Kenite be; blessed shall she be above women in the tent. He asked water, & she gave him milk; she brought forth butter in a lordly dish. She put her hand to the nail, & her right hand to the workmen's hammer; & with the hammer she smote Sisera, she smote off his head, when she had pierced & stricken through his temples. At her feet he bowed, he fell, he lay down: at her feet he bowed, he fell: where he bowed, there he fell down dead.'

"Makes sense so far. Deborah rejoices because Jael did the Lord's work, killing Sisera, king of Hazor, who conquered the Israelites & oppressed them for 20 yrs.

" 'So let all thine enemies perish, O Lord!' the prophetess sings—but only at the end, in her last verse (31), after she tells us:

" 'The mother of Sisera looked out at a window & cried through the lattice, Why is his chariot so long in coming? why tarry the wheels of his chariots? Her wise ladies answered her, yea, she returned answer to herself. Have they not sped? have they not divided the prey; to every man a damsel or two; to Sisera a prey of divers colors, a prey of divers colors of needlework, of divers colors of needlework on both sides, meet for the necks of them that take the spoil?'

"In other words, her maid servants try to get her mind off her son. They jabber about the plunder Sisera will bring back. A girl or two for every man! Two lengths of dyed cloth for Sisera—embroidered on both sides!

"But Sisera's dead! His poor Ma! We ain't told her name. But we pity her. That's why Deborah sings about her! Because God wants us to feel pity, even for Sisera's Ma. Was she not also created by Him?

"God has delivered the Del. of Greentown into your hands. They are His children. Pity them! Think of the old lady looking thro' that latticed window."

Lambright, who was drunk, said, "Ain't life grand?"

Told me he buried his 4 daughters in Pitts. under a single tombstone, on which he carved,

> One sire, one womb
> Their being gave.
> They shared a sickness
> And now this grave.

Sam Lewis & son butchered the 4 razorbacks the former stole from Greentown for tonight's roast. My first taste of pork in 3 yrs.!

7 Sept.

With the Rev., in the ravine, Mans. 132 Del. men, women & children are encamped here under guard.

Bowl Woman's 12 day old son, Pet-hak-al-lune (Thunder Arrow) died of dysentery yesterday afternoon. Buried near the blockhouse.

Armstrong's son, Silas, speaks English. He is Kratzer's interpreter, takes roll call of his people every eve. in return for 1 gall. whisky daily.

8 Sept.

Beam's blockhouse. 7 PM. Raining.

1½ months since my last drink.

Sarah & Sam Lewis, Jr. eye but won't speak with each other. Her fair hair is too wiry, nose too thick, but she has spunk, intelligence. Learned to read from her father's copy, "Book of Martyrs."

Chapman reading "Heaven & Hell."

Old man Seymour's wife, Leah, was 3 months pregnant when drowned by Indians in the Mad River.

"You never told me that, Pa!" says Phil.

Last night, near the gate, I overheard Martha working on Billy to abandon his wife & kids: "The Lord provides, and them He joins together, let no man put ass-under. He gave you me! Your wife come here, and you ain't never gonna put your paws on my tits again!"

Lettiece: "If them Injuns busts in here amongst us, shoot me, Massa Tom."

"I promise."

"Thank you, Massa!"

11 PM. Snores, groans, fleas, the smell of sweat. Neither Fanny nor I could sleep. We talked by the well.

"Your paintings scare me, Tom. But I like them. That picture of Tommy Lyons, in particular. He looks sad."

"Forty-four dollars! You're a good businessman, too. But I must tell you, I don't approve of profits from a Still. Once we're wed, you must give it up. I have money of my own put by. Twenty-two dollars. Plus my cabin and land—Henry and me bought 20 prime acres with the other half of my dowry."

9 Sept. 1 PM.

In the ravine, with Pru & the Rev. He has just been asked by Silas to intervene with Kratzer. "Tell him, let my people go to Upper Piqua. Otherwise, more will die of the shits. My father is sick."

The mud!

Bowl Woman has painted her face black. Her husband is on the war-path with Tommy Lyons.

2:15 PM. Central Park blockhouse. Capt. Douglas, Bob Coffinberry, et al. returned here early this morn. They tracked Jones' murderers to Upper Sandusky, where the trail got cold.

Bob: "Douglas didn't think it safe to come back the same way we went, so we come through Frederickstown. We fired off our guns in a salute on the street. Two women fainted. Everybody else run for the blockhouse. They took us for redskins! I could of got shot!"

Kratzer: "We march, Sunday, at dawn!"

6 PM. Beam's blockhouse.

We informed Silas of the above. He offered the Rev. 2 otter skins worth $4.00 for Pru. "I can eat a dog I do not know."

The Rev. said, "I can't allow her to be eaten."

"My father says that close to the end of the world, there will be a sign. All dogs' noses will drop off."

10 Sept. 11 PM.

Beam's. Fanny asked me this eve. about life at Blue Hill. "Were you happy?"

"Not at the time, no. But looking back, I was. Yes. (!)"

"Are you happy, now?"

"Are you?"

"Yes."

"Me, too."

"I'll make you a good wife, Tom."

Fanny,
I will make thee

Over in my bed.
Eventually,
We three
Will ply there.
Yes, why not?
Lettiece agrees.
I see it in her eyes.
      (11:15 PM)

11 Sept. 9 PM.

Beam's. The warrior named Toby & his 11 year old daughter, Flower Beginning to Bloom Woman (Mau-nou-goke-co), escaped from Mans. during this morn.'s storm. Silas betrayed them to Kratzer for 1½ gall. whisky as soon as he discovered they were missing. Bob & Phil resolved to track the Indians down.

6 miles out, on the Upper Sandusky trail, they overtook & fired upon them, wounding Toby in the back of the neck. He ran about 40 rods to a stream, drank, then collapsed beside it under a cottonwood. Flower Beginning to Bloom Woman disappeared in a thick cane brake. Bob & Phil returned to town, told what they had done & split a jug. About 3 PM, Kratzer dispatched them & 5 militiamen under Jethro Stone to make sure Toby was dead.

They found him sitting against the tree with his breechclout wrapped around his neck. Bob & Phil dismounted. Bob drew his tomahawk from his belt & handed it to Phil, saying,

"Take revenge for your drownded Ma!"

Stone yelled, "Don't!"

Toby raised his right hand, crying, "En-gau-has!" (Mama!)

Phil buried the tomahawk up to its handle into Toby's neck, under his left ear. Some blood from the severed artery squirted into Phil's mouth. Stone & his men covered the corpse with logs, then everyone came here to dine upon roasted venison, courtesy of Lambright, & "Ma's" Johnny cakes.

Phil is smoking the little clay pipe he took from a fringed buckskin bag round Toby's neck. Told me that before burning the Council House at Greentown, he & the 8 militiamen—one after the other—pissed on the floor.

Bob, who inherited all of Jones' property, says, "Levi should a knowed more than to leave young Cooper's grave first. Soon as I seed him do it, I says to myself, 'Jonesy, you're a goner. You're done for. They'll tuck you under next. And nobody but your booby of a self to blame for it.' "

12 Sept. 11 PM.
Beam's. Bob & Phil got drunk again this morn., returned to corpse. Uncovered, scalped & beheaded it. Phil carried the head in his knapsack to Central Park, where Bob stuck it on a pole. He then filled the scalp with whisky & drank it, mixed with blood. So did Phil & Kratzer.

Stone threw the scalp on a fire & brought the boys hither about 6 o'clock.

13 Sept. Sun. 7 AM.
Bought of Bob Coffinberry at his store, Mans.,
6 black lead pencils.. $1.15.
Bought of the above, 1 mock garnet brooch ...... .67.
    "   "   "   , 10 lbs. of deer tallow,
@ .05 per lb. .... .50.

The last item—plunder from Greentown—was half the usual price.

10 AM. The Rev. atop the oaken stump in Central Park:
"In Psalm 89, verse 46, Ethan the Ezrahite, asks, 'How long Lord? wilt thou hide thyself for ever?' I answer, 'Christ comes today! We must be reborn! That means nothing less than always to begin again!' "

He burst out crying. Beam ended the Meeting with the hymn,

What is this that casts you down?
"   "   " that grieves you?
Speak & let the worst be known.
Speaking may relieve you.

Beam much relieved that Billy & Martha have parted company. The former will return tomorrow to his bachelor's hall & get it ready for his wife & kids, who must arrive Mans. before the first snow.

11 AM. Williams' Tavern. Kratzer & 12 mounted militiamen will presently conduct 129 Del. SSW. thro' Berkshire Twp., & cross Elm Creek in Delaware (!) County to Upper Piqua—125 miles.

Supplies: 17 barrels of salt, 6 doz. of fish, 3 doz. of flour, 3 doz. of wheat, 2 doz. of pork, & a considerable quantity of dry corn & beans. Capt. Douglas, Jethro Stone & 9 others will man the Central Park blockhouse till Kratzer returns on or about 9 Oct.

Bowl Woman died last night of the cholera; buried in an unmarked grave near her son behind the Central Park blockhouse. Armstrong refuses to bid the Rev. farewell.

Toby's head has no eyes (crows).

11 PM. Beam's blockhouse. At 2 o'clock, Armstrong told Kratzer, "We're ready to leave," & mounted his bay mare. The few other Del. horsemen did the same. Such as were riding in wagons seated themselves. Most were afoot.

Armstrong commanded 4 musicians to flank him at the head of his people, saying, "Cheer us up!"

One beat a drum; three played upon cedar flutes.

A girl clutching her belly. An old man with leg ulcers. A naked female lunatick, about my age, led by 2 men.

14 Sept.

Beam's blockhouse. Rain during the night. Morn. cloudy & sultry with a brisk SW. wind.

Fanny thanked me for the brooch. She's worried about the Rev., who suffers from nausea, palpitations, the night sweats. He's returning home with his family later this afternoon.

I will do likewise. Geo. Coffinberry, who last visited my place Sat., says blackbirds are in the corn.

Phil furious. Martha & Billy are back together. Chapman told them,

"Man's life don't change after death. Adulterers live in brothels forever."

He explained that according to Swedenborg, these brothels are in the W. quarter of Hell, at the edge of a dark forest. The adulterers fornicate in their own excrement.

2 PM. Jethro Stone hither with news brought him by Dan Russel from Chillicothe: Tecumseh has roused all the Indian nations of the NW., save the Del., against us. On 3 Sept., at Pigeon Roost, in southern Indiana, a big war party killed & scalped 3 men, 5 women & 16 children. Fort Wayne is besieged.

Everyone remaining here. Lambright has ordered Phil & Beam to join Chapman as scouts.

15 Sept.

Beam's blockhouse. Phil, Beam & Chapman (unarmed) left afoot at 4 AM to scout WNW. for 1½ days.

Lambright & I will harvest C.'s apples in his Owl Creek nursery. Beth still won't tell him why he must plant apple trees throughout the NW. Territory. She also made him plant dog-fennel (*Foeniculum vulgate* L.) as a cure for intermittent fever, but changed her mind about 5 yrs. ago. No reason given.

C. told me that while visiting his Ma's grave behind the Longmeadow (Mass.) Meeting house at about 7 PM, on Wed. 13 Jan. 1790, Beth whispered for the first time into his left ear, saying,

"I'm your Ma's best friend in Heaven."

He ran the ½ mile home on his snow-shoes. 2 days later, he was making nails in the kitchen when Beth whispered in the same ear,

"Your Ma sends you her love. We got the same Christian name—Elizabeth. Call me Beth."

Stone, whose horse has thrown a shoe, buried Toby's head this morn. in Central Park.

While Fanny nursed Carrie behind a blanket hung in a corner, Stone said,

"One time in Clinton County, Pa., a gal fetched a babe 10 mile to see Doc Swatsworth in Lock Haven, saying, 'He's losing weight.'

"Doc examined the babe, then asked the gal about her victuals, but she says, 'What I eat got nothing to do with little Johnny here being so skinny.'

Doc figured she must be kinda dumb, so he didn't ask no more questions. He opened her bodice to see if there was something wrong with her tits. Then he sucked first one and then the other. There wasn't no milk in either. She says,

" 'Johnny's my sister's babe, Doc!'

"The doc says, 'Then why'd you come?'

" 'I didn't,' says she, 'till you started sucking the second one.' "

Said I, "You're a Dutchman, Jethro Stone!"

"You're right," says he. "My Pa's name was Stein. How did you know?"

"I spent almost eight years working for Dutchmen in Pennsylvania. You're the only folks I know who use the word dumb that way; meaning not mute but stupid."

"By Christ! I never thought of that! It's probably because in German the word for stupid is 'dummkopf.' "

Bob showed me the contents of the medicine bag Toby wore about his neck: 2 bear claws, a tuft of bear fur, an otter's nose, 2 blue ribbons & an eagle's head.

18 Sept.

Beam's blockhouse. 9 AM. In the last 2 days, Lambright, Sam Lewis, Jr., & I have picked, then hauled hither by sled, 60 bushels of C.'s apples, which the women are boiling down for butter.

The smell of the mash made Juno try twice to poke her muzzle into Mrs. Coffinberry's copper kettle. Also attracted by the smell—hornets. One stung the back of Sarah's hand as she stirred the mash.

Carrie is passing loose green stools.

Noon. Beam just returned. He scouted W. along Broken Sword Creek, within 10 miles of Indian Territory, toward Upper Sandusky. "No sign of 'em."

12:30. Fanny gave Carrie a gentle vomit of ipercacuanha.

2 PM. Phil has arrived, a red kerchief about his head. He scouted the trail NW toward old Fort Miami. "There's no redskins in that neck of the woods."

2:15 PM. The same news from Chapman, who scouted N. toward Sandusky Bay, via New Haven, then followed the boundary of the Western Reservation to the headwaters of the W. branch of the Upper Huron. C. said, "Caleb Palmer forgave me for last month's false alarm. Had me to supper in New Haven. His Mrs. makes a savory Plymouth Rock pudding."

3 PM. Fanny dosed Carrie with rhubarb to mitigate the acrimony of her humors. Stool still loose & green.

9 PM. Carrie asleep.

Everybody returning home at dawn. By a vote of 13 to 1, we will give all 10 lbs. of apple butter to the boys in the Central Park blockhouse. The Rev. said, "Don't! They're thieves!"

Jethro Stone once confessed to him that the militiamen will share equally from an auction to be held next month in Mt. Vernon of Del. goods; the peltry alone is worth $600–900.

We agreed by unanimous acclaim that Sam & Geo., living nearest to Greentown, are to share between themselves as they see fit all the Del. crops.

11 PM. Carrie now passes normal stools.

Fanny set our wedding date: Mon., 12 Oct. (Her Pa's birthday.)

19 Sept. Sat.
Spent all morn. cleaning my cabin after its occupation for almost 3 wks. by squirrels & coons. The former piled walnuts, hickorys & acorns in a corner of the hanging cupboard. The latter pried open my blanket chest, scattered everything within, & chewed my frilled shirt, woolen cap, coat's hood & new stockings. They also gnawed the hoe handle. Etc. Etc. Etc.

This afternoon, began picking my corn—the inexplicable yellow gourdseed. A goodly crop.

21 Sept. 11 PM.
Beam's blockhouse.
Martha, Billy & old man Seymour were tomahawked while digging potatoes yesterday afternoon. The Rev., coming to call, saw the corpses in the potato patch from the trail. Frightened that Indians were hiding in the cabin, he rode back home, warned his family, then fetched Phil & me. We added Lambright, Sam & Geo. to our numbers.

By the time we arrived at the Seymours', it was early eve. The Rev., with his sawed-off rifle, crept around to the back window, listened a moment, then crept to the door, which was ajar. The cabin was empty.

The corpses were scalped & disemboweled. Old man Seymour's & Billy's cocks were in their mouths. Martha's breasts were skinned. They are made by Indians into bullet pouches, says Beam.

Old man Seymour's Still was smashed. The Indians stole Sadie & Julia, the 2 mares, & cut out the tongue of Potiphar, the ox, who bled to death in his stall. They also stole old man Seymour's rifle, Billy's musket, & all their powder & shot. In addition to the meal sack & Martha's pocket looking-glass.

We buried her with Billy & her Pa in one grave on the knoll. The Rev. declined to say a few words of his own at the funeral.

We hastened to his cabin. The door was barred & windows made fast. Mrs. Cooper was armed with her son's musket, Lettiece with an axe. Likewise, Mrs. Lambright, whom we picked up on the way—a broad axe. The Coffinberry family was at the Lewises', where we all remained in the cabin with Juno till dawn, when we fled here.

22 Sept.

Beam's blockhouse. 5 AM.

About an hr. ago, Phil, drunk & weeping, cried out, "I'm an orphan!"

Chapman, still unarmed, back from the Seymours'. He estimates that there were 5–7 Indians with 3–5 horses in the war party. They rode into the creek bed, where their track was lost.

Lambright believes that the warriors burned neither cabin nor corn lest the smoke give them away.

To be on the safe side, we will pick & haul everyone's corn here.

Have a sore throat.

6 AM.   Phil (still drunk), Beam & Chapman gone to scout Upper Sandusky; they agree with Lambright, who reckons that the raiding party came from one of the British-Indian encampments on the W. shore of Lake Erie.

Once again, before leaving, Chapman spoke with me about Beth Holland. She told him about her big nose & ample bosom late one afternoon in June, '91, while he was picking strawberries with his 10 half-brothers & sisters. None of them heard her. Thereafter, she whispered to him at least twice a month for 7 yrs.

"Sometimes, she hummed, 'Holy, Holy, Holy.' Judge Homer Young of Greensburg, in Westmoreland County, Pa., saved my sanity. I was his hired man at the time—September, '98.

"One night he told me he belonged to the Church of the New Jerusalem; that it was founded by followers of the great

Swedish natural scientist Emanuel Swedenborg, who preaches that we don't die but exchange our natural bodies for spiritual ones.

"I asked, 'And do these Spirits ever reveal themselves to men?'

" 'Often,' says he. 'It happened to Swedenborg all the time. He calls it a vastation.'

" 'A vastation,' said I. 'Has it happened to you?'

" 'No,' says he. 'Alas!'

"I stayed up till dawn reading Young's copy of 'Heaven and Hell.' At breakfast, I told him about Beth. He cried out,

" 'God be praised! She's your Guardian Angel! You must obey her in everything!'

"That evening, in the parlor, Beth commanded me to plant apple trees and dog-fennel all over the NW. Territory and never eat meat. I told the Judge. There was a pork roast for supper. His wife fixed me buckwheat cakes. Next month, he lent me, without interest, the $120 I needed to buy my first nursery. It's on Big Brokenstraw Creek, near White's, in Warren County, Pa. White's son, Pete, looks after it for me."

11 PM. Beam's. The (drunken) militiamen in Mans. this afternoon wouldn't lend us a hand with Jones', Williams', Bob Coffinberry's—or anyone's—corn. They obviously wanted us to offer them a bribe. Said Capt. Douglas,

"These boys are serving Ohio for only ten bucks a month."

"Fuck 'em," said Lambright. "You, too!"

Douglas: "Watch what you say about Ohio!"

Lambright divided us into 6 pickers & 2 loader-haulers—myself and Williams, a good teamster. We made 2 trips hither in Williams' ox cart, carrying a total of 35 bushels.

Not enough. Lettiece, Delight Coffinberry, Hattie Lambright, Mrs. Cooper & Grace Lewis have volunteered to join the pickers in Mans. tomorrow. Sam & Bob will drive—& guard—the latter's cart & yoke of oxen.

Dan Russel arrived on a blown horse about 9 PM with Williams' & old man Seymour's copy of "The Fredonian."

He will return to Chillicothe tomorrow morn., bearing a letter to Billy's widow in Cincinnati from the Rev. He can't fall asleep till first light.

Sam Lewis, Jr. teaching Sarah to play "Yankee Doodle" upon his fife.

Two months without a drink. Have taken up cigars.

23 Sept.

Beam's blockhouse. Slight rain & fog this morn. Now (11 PM) warm & damp with a gentle NE. wind.

80 bushels in 4 trips from Mans. today; ditto, Sam & Bob. Oxen frantic from black jaws, against which Williams & I smear bear grease on our exposed parts.

My sore throat better.

Tomorrow we start working our way down the Black Fork.

A relief force reached the seventy-man garrison of Fort Wayne on 12 Sept., after a 6 day siege; the Indians had fled. Their British reinforcements never showed—"The Fredonian."

Foreign Intelligence: on 24 June, Napoleon invaded Russia. The emperor himself led the attack on the city of Vilna.

24 Sept.   9:30 PM.

Beam's. Phil, Beam & Chapman returned about 2 o'clock from the main fork of the Sandusky River with the broken blade of a new scalping knife stamped with the mark "Jukes Coulson & Co." British made!

Chapman discovered it at an abandoned Indian encampment—45 (!) holes, dug in the earth, where small hardwood fires had been lit to prevent their being seen.

Capt. Douglas & Jethro Stone joined us for dinner. The latter said the above number means nothing; Indians on the war-path build as many fires as possible to scare their enemies.

All we can surmise is that a raiding party of undetermined size crossed Miami Bay in canoes from British territory on the W. shore of Lake Erie; that it made its way from

Sandusky Bay to the Sandusky River & then S. to Mans. We are in danger as long as the good weather holds—Indian summer. Stone, C., Beam & Phil will coordinate their efforts to reconnoiter the neighborhood.

Drunken Phil curses himself for being vexed by his father's demand that he be fed his corn mush exactly at noon.

Stone has no family. One of the reasons he enjoys being a scout—vivid dreams. "I only remember my dreams whilst sleeping in a different place every night."

25 Sept. Fri.

Beam's blockhouse. Heavy rain all afternoon, while we brought in 120 bushels my corn. At 9 PM, cloudy with a strong NW. wind.

The Rev. gave a good deal of thought to yellow gourdseed corn this past year.

"It don't violate Scripture 'cause it ain't a new kind of plant! It's a variety of one already created!"

He must take laudanum to sleep. Two nights ago, he threw his Journal—3 vols., including 156 (!) sermons—onto the fire in the stockade. "I made God a burnt offering."

Our scouts report no sign of Indians within a six-mile radius of Mans.

A second blockhouse is being built in Central Park by 24 militiamen of the 3rd Reg., 2nd Brigade, 3rd Div., under Capt. Erik Shaffer, who arrived with them from Coshocton this morn. He dined with us on roasted venison. 26, reddish hair, watery blue eyes set close together. Carved upon his powder horn: "Erik Shaffer His Horn Made Sept. 30th 1811. I Powder with my Brother Ball a Hearoe Like to Conquer All."

Shaffer tells us that within the last 2 wks., blockhouses were built & garrisoned by State militiamen all along the frontier—at Fredericktown & Clinton (Knox Co.). Also Belville, Wooster & Jeromeville. Thom. Coulter's cabin, near Perryville, was fortified.

"Everyone's scared that Tecumseh has loosed his hordes upon us."

Shaffer learned about "the Seymour massacre" 3 days ago—a dispatch rider from Van Meter's.

Brig. Gen. Reasin Beall of New Lisbon, Columbiana Co., is raising a brigade of State militia (about 2000 men) in Canton. Mansfield is on his line of march to Lower Sandusky, where Gen. Harrison awaits fresh supplies & reinforcements.

We have agreed to supply daily & without charge to Capt. Shaffer 3 gills of cracked corn each for his 8 horses. In exchange, beginning tomorrow, he will send us 10 pickers till the harvest is in—Mon. noon, at the latest, including 300–350 bushels from Greentown.

11 PM. Indians.

Indian corn—all varieties—tobacco & poison ivy.

Also beavers, raccoons, rattlesnakes, opossums, turkeys, woodchucks, buffaloes, etc.

They are indigenous only to this Continent.

How did they get here?

Were they on Noah's Ark?

Then why are they not found in other parts of the world?

Were they created separately?

26 Sept. 10 AM.

Beam's.

At dawn, a charge of gunpowder blew apart the stockade gate. A score of howling savages—faces & hands painted red—rushed inside & shot everybody around the breakfast fire—Williams, Geo. Coffinberry & Sam Lewis, Jr.

Geo.'s dogs were with him but gave no warning; he fell dead in the flames. Williams' lower jaw was shattered. I saw a fat redskin brain him with a tomahawk. I heard the skull crack. Sam Lewis, Jr., who was frying some venison, took a musket ball in the fleshy part of the right thigh, below the hip.

Tommy Lyons scalped the boy alive, then cut his throat

from ear to ear, down to the neckbone, and dumped the corpse into the well.

Smoke, screams, musketry. During the next 20 mins., I got off 6 rounds. Hit nobody. Lambright & Beam, who were firing thro' the portholes on my right, killed 2 each. Bob blew the back of the head off Little Bear running for cover behind the shed. Phil wounded another warrior in the knee; he went down in front of the blockhouse.

The Rev. opened the door, crying, "He's mine!"

But before he could shoot, a rifle ball struck his chest, severing the strap of his powder horn. Beam barred the door. The Rev. dropped his gun & staggered back. I caught him in my arms.

Thus I was present when he looked up at his wife & asked, "Ma, are you praying that this cup should pass from me?"

"Yes, Ezra."

He said, "Don't. I'm so happy."

His lips turned blue; he couldn't catch his breath. He vomited blood. Mrs. Cooper wiped his mouth with a yellow kerchief. The death-rattle began; he soiled himself. She shut his eyes.

Sarah shrieked, "Pa, I'm to blame. Forgive me!"

The Indians drove off our horses and slashed the bellies of the 2 cows & 9 oxen in the stockade. I saw Mike, one of Williams' Red Devons, trip over his own entrails. The cries sounded human; Chapman clapped his hands over his ears.

It took a minute or two before any of us in the blockhouse realized the Indians were gone. They'd fled at the approach on the trail from Mans. of Shaffer's 10 militiamen.

Jethro Stone accompanied them on horseback. "I knowed there was trouble."

He was awakened last night by an owl hooting in Central Park. "That means death."

He dragged Geo.'s half-charred corpse from the fire by one foot. Sam Lewis pulled his dead boy from the bloody well. I put Juno out of her misery, quenched my thirst in the creek, & wrote the above.

1 PM. The place still stinks of blood, gunpowder & burned
paper cartridges.

Jethro Stone says our attackers retreated with their dead
& wounded. "Gone north-northwest, thro' the weeds on the
other side of the creek, above the mill."

Lambright posted 5 militiamen as pickets, despite a protest
from their drunken Irish sgt., whom we've nicknamed "I'm
in Command Here."

Lettiece: "It's good to be in the land of the livin'! Specially
when you think of them that ain't!"

7 PM.
Bought of Bob Coffinberry, 1 lb. pig tail
tobacco .... .14.
Bought of the above, 4 lbs. salt .... .25.

This afternoon, we buried the Rev. Ezra Cooper (aged
50), Geo. Coffinberry (36), Isaac Williams (32) & Sam Lewis
Jr. (14 years, 2 months) in one grave at the foot of the apple
tree a few rods S. of the shattered gate.

Beam conducted the Methodist funeral. At Fanny's request,
I recited Num. 6:24–26 in Hebrew & English:

$$\text{יְבָרֶכְךָ֥ יְהֹוָ֖ה וְיִשְׁמְרֶֽךָ׃}$$

etc.

The Lord bless thee, and keep thee:
The Lord make his face shine upon thee,
    and be gracious unto thee:
The Lord lift up his countenance upon thee,
    and give thee peace.

Beam then said, "This here's for Sam Jr.," & played
"Yankee Doodle" upon his fife.

Sam Sr. said, "My boy wanted to be the first President of
the United States from Ohio."

I skinned & salted down Juno's hide; gave the liver to

Jethro Stone, who roasted it on a forked stick for his supper. We're all abashed by our appetites. I ate 3 helpings of Fanny's fried corn.

Told Mrs. Cooper, "Ezra was a Christian. I'm an infidel. If I were a Christian, I'd want to be as good a one as he."

27 Sept.

Cleaned our weapons & kept watch all night. No sleep. At first light, made our way afoot 2½ miles up the Rocky Fork to Kratzer's blockhouse, Mans., now under Lambright's command.

Delight Coffinberry asked Bob to remove her & her 3 sons, aged 2½–7, to Xenia, in Greene Co., where her Pa owns a saw-mill.

Bob: "That means hauling you over a hundred miles thro' woods swarming with savages. I won't do it!"

Terror made me jerk rather than squeeze my trigger & shoot high during yesterday's fight. I have a vivid memory of Lambright calmly smoking a cigar as he rammed a ball into the breech of his Lancaster Co. rifle. Says he,

"My arse-hole puckered up. I was that scared. All I thought about was—'Will I live or will I die?' and once in a while, 'Poor Hattie! Suppose them savages get their hands on her?' Also, 'This ain't really happening.'"

I worried about Carrie & Fanny under a pile of bedclothes in the corner behind the ladder.

28 Sept.

Mans. From last Wed.'s "Fredonian":

Mount Vernon: A family has been lately murdered by Indians, six miles from Greentown (a Delaware village about 50 miles northeast of this place, on the waters of the Black Fork of Mohecan John's Creek), consisting of a Mr. Walter Seymour, his daughter, and a hired man of the name of William Stump.

The Murders were committed by a small party of disaffected Greentown Indians who refused to accompany

Chief Armstrong and the rest of their tribe to Upper Piqua. Greentown has since been burned down by the whites.

Phil miffed that Martha's not mentioned by name.

This morn. Bob took over Williams' Tavern, henceforth to be called "The Liberty Tree," which I agreed to supply with whisky, of 80 proof, @ .45 per gall. &—for $4.00 upon delivery—a painted sign of my design.

Our corn was picked too early. Lest it molder, we must immediately husk and haul it from Beam's to the crib being built between the 2 blockhouses in Central Park. Jethro Stone has taken it upon himself to fetch the necessary carts & yokes from Mt. Vernon.

Tonight, Mrs. Cooper said to me, "Life goes on as usual. I hate it."

Beam promised to take her, Sarah, Lettiece & Pru to the Rev.'s younger brother, Hiram, a cabinet maker, in Cincinnati.

Asked Sarah why she blamed herself for her Pa's death; she burst into tears.

29 Sept.
Bought of Bob Coffinberry, at his store, Mans.,
1 toilet looking-glass .... .28.

This eve., Lettiece told Mrs. Cooper, "I won't go back to Cincinnati. The Rev., he promised to take me to Canada after the war. Massa Johnny be my witness."

C.: "Tis true. I pledge myself to carry out that oath."

Fanny: "That makes it my Christian duty to go with Ma and Sarah and get them settled. You come fetch me in the spring, Tom. We'll get married then."

"Whatever you say."

Lettiece here alone all winter!

9 PM. Fanny: "Lettiece took me by surprise, Tom. I didn't mean to be abrupt with you. Nor take advantage. But I can't desert Ma. Maybe, if I do my Christian duty by her

in Cincinnati till spring, God won't punish me for marrying an infidel."

9:30 PM. Bob: "Down home in Albemarle Co., Va., there was a mulatto gal named Rose who thrice tried running away. She also wanted to live in Canada. Whuppings didn't stop her, so her mistress—Lucy Daniels—belled her. An iron hoop was welded round her waist, another about her neck, and attached to these, a long rod went up her back. A bell was hung from it, beyond her reach, over head. It rang every time she moved."

30 Sept.

Bought from Bob Coffinberry at his store,
Mans., 1 lb. pig tail tobacco ....   .14.

This morn. foggy, slight rain, gentle SE. wind. At 8 PM, clear & fine.

Sarah's 12th birthday; clutches her Pa's powder horn. I gave her the looking-glass. Said she, "I can't stand to look at my face."

Gave Lambright tobacco. Today also his birthday (55). Mentioned the coincidence to Fanny, who said, "You never asked my age, Tom. Come Jan. 19th, I'll be 23. How 'bout you?"

When I replied, "I'm 20 years older than you," she looked taken aback, then pleased. Delight Coffinberry, who was ironing her apron, said,

"George and I are—were—the same age."

Grace Lewis has been drunk since the funeral.

Yankee pot roast for supper; we talked about the battle at Beam's.

Sam Lewis: "I took good aim from the upstairs window at Tommy Lyons, and fired, but he saw the flash in my pan and throwed himself down. The ball passed over him. By the time I loaded again, he was gone."

Phil had resolved to turn the blunderbuss on Sarah if the Indians broke down the blockhouse door. Bob blew off the back of Little Bear's head with a musket ball transfixed by a 2″ nail—a hunter's trick, which inflicts a huge wound.

Phil & Bob are now rich. Beam cited Deut. 25:5 & urged Bob to marry Delight. Said Bob,

"I will if she'll have me."

"I wanna go home to Pa," said Delight.

Lettiece won't return to Cincinnati because she's scared of being kidnapped there by "nigger stealers," taken across the Ohio to Kentucky & sold off.

Lettiece—
Your ruined mouth
Arouses me.
Would that we
Could spend nights
South.
There would I
Your Master be
Till dawn sets
You at liberty.
Who will free
My Soul sold South,
Cried off by your
Ruined mouth?

11 PM. This Sun. (4 Oct.), Mrs. Cooper will sell her lands, goods, chattels, & 140 bushels of corn at auction & depart for Cincinnati.

Fanny said to me, "We must make a 225 mile trip thro' woods infested with painted savages. By ox cart and flat boat. One old man, two women, a 7½ month old babe in arms, a 12 year old girl, and a silly hound dog.

"You were magnificent at Beam's, Tom! Face blackened with gunpowder, blood-shot eyes. I watched you take aim. You bared your teeth! Come with us to Cincinnati, Tom. Protect us. I beg you!"

"Yes, of course."

The drunken Irish sgt. ("I'm in Command Here") tried

to sell me life insurance. He's an agent of the N. American Insurance Co., Philadelphia.

1 Oct.

Bought in Mans. of Otto Fischer from Mt. Vernon, "Gen. Wayne," a bright bay gelding, 4 years old, a star in his forehead, white hind feet, 13½ hands high .... $25.00.

I have in ready money .... 16.07.

Fischer—he speaks broken English—one of 8 teamsters who arrived this afternoon with Jethro Stone. They brought their carts, yokes, 12 horses, divers goods, including a 50 gall. Still & news that Gen. Beall yesterday dispatched to us one company of riflemen from his encampment in Stark Co.

Bob and Delight are getting "The Liberty Tree" ready for business.

Tonight, Sarah confessed to me that late in the afternoon of 25 Sept., the day before the attack, she wandered into the corn field W. of the stockade & saw an Indian behind a brush heap at the edge of the woods.

"Next time I looked, the Injun was gone. I didn't tell Pa 'cause he was very strict in regard to the truth. He would of skinned me alive for raising a false alarm."

2 Oct. Fri.

Early this morn., accompanied by Phil & Jethro Stone, Fanny, Hattie Lambright & Lettiece went to do laundry at the run N. of Diamond St., Mans. A dozen Indians, including Tommy Lyons, attacked them as Lettiece unloaded the kettle from the ox cart. Phil, who drove the team, was shot in the left eye & fell forward to the ground. Tommy Lyons jumped off his horse. He made a circular cut around the crown of Phil's skull and pulled off the scalp with his teeth.

At the same instant, Jethro Stone took cover on the bank behind the dead cottonwood, where he faced about & fired at Tommy Lyons, but missed. Another mounted warrior, taking advantage of Stone's empty rifle, charged him from the rear. Stone faced about again, drew his tomahawk. The horse knocked him into the water. Fanny left her hiding place in the small timber to pull him out. They were taken prisoner. Hattie & Lettiece escaped via the ravine, returned here (Kratzer's blockhouse), from whence Lambright dispatched 2 parties in pursuit.

I rode N. with the first for 5 miles; finding ourselves separated from the others, under Lambright, who were afoot, & being only 4 in number, we returned to Mans. about 2 PM. An hour later, the second party, having come upon the tracks of 5–6 unshod horses near Quaker Springs, returned also.

Lambright said, "There was no way we could overtake 'em."

We buried Phil where he died. 32 years old. Yesterday he said to me, "It ain't enough to get rich; your friends must stay poor."

Chapman, out scouting on his own, returned before 5 o'clock with 4 sharpened quills the size of rye straws, which he found sticking up among those tracks near Quaker Springs. He says their points were dipped by the Indians in rattlesnake venom.

(Lambright: "I didn't see 'em. Christ Almighty! I could of got killed!")

Said C., "I know these heathen and their tricks. I lived among them at Greentown in 1809 for 9 months. I speak their language. They worship evil spirits. I know all about them, too."

He victualed himself with a small quantity of boiled corn & beans, then borrowed Gen. Wayne from me, saying,

"Tommy Lyons owes me. He calls me 'En-naughk'—'My Father'—for the favor I done him last December, when his Pa died. Believe it or not, your Indian is a man of honor. He might free Fanny and Jethro for me.

"If I ain't back in a week, notify Judge Homer Young, 'The Willows,' Greensburg, Westmoreland Co., Penn. He's been like a father to me."

11 PM.   Lettiece weaning Carrie to Indian pudding—corn mush mixed with water and molasses.

Early this eve., while fetching logs to replace the stockade gate, I thought I saw Fanny in her blue bodice standing under the red cedar on Main St.

11:30 PM.
Bought of Bob Coffinberry, at "The Liberty
Tree," Mans., 1 qt. Madeira wine .... $2.25.

3 Oct.

Slept it off under oaken table, "The Liberty Tree."

At 2 PM: the shakes, headache, nausea, burning stomach & what Lambright calls "privy mouth."

2:30 PM.   Hair of the dog that bit me.

Beam says that C. left his 2 nurseries in Penn. & 5 in Ohio valued in excess of $1200 to Judge Young to publish Emanuel Swedenborg's works & spread his "Heavenly Doctrine" throughout the NW. Territory.

Lambright: "Chapman made me promise to look after Lettiece and make sure she gets to Canada when the war's over."

10 PM.
Sold tonight to Capt. Daniel Blunt, on his own
Company of mounted Riflemen, 1st Regt., 3rd
Detachment, Ohio Militia, 60 bushels of my
corn, @ .40 per bushel, for which I have his
receipt-in-hand, promising Gen. Beall to pay me
in one month .... $24.00.

He & his Company of 60 officers & men are in advance of Gen. Beall, encamped for these last 3 weeks with 2000 troops & 25 cannon at Bethlehem Twp., Stark Co., on the Tuscarawas.

"No man in Ohio is more aptly named—'Blunt.' For that's what I am, Mr. Keene—a blunt soldier.

"I heard what happened yesterday morning to your betrothed. You must expect the worst. The summer of '79, I was serving as an Ensign with Col. Morgan's Rifle Battalion at a fort on the Monongahela in Westmoreland Co., Penn. A Canasadaga war party captured twin 16 year old sisters— Maria and Christine Manheim—while they was chopping nettles in their Pa's corn near Muddy Creek.

"Two weeks later, one of our spies—a half-breed named Jim Killbuck—come to the fort and told us what the Canasadaga done to the girls in a pine swamp.

"Some of them pruned two saplings of branches and cleared away all the brush for several rods around. The rest split pitch pine sticks into hundreds and hundreds of splinters, each as thick as your little finger, but about six inches long. Then they sharpened them at one end and dipped the other in boiling resin.

"They stripped the girls and tied them to the saplings with their hands above their heads. They stuck the hundreds and hundreds of sharpened splinters into them, from their knees to their shoulders. And then the splinters, all sticking out of the bleeding flesh, were set on fire. The girls took three hours to die."

11 PM.
Bought of Bob Coffinberry, "The Liberty
Tree," Mans., 1 qt. Madeira wine..................... $2.25.

5 Oct.   Mon.
Bought of Bob Coffinberry, at his store Mans.,
1 pair spectacles... 1.00.

A replacement for the pair lost during my 24 hour bender, about which I remember nothing. Lambright found me unconscious back of the corn crib at sunup.

He calls the 1st Regt. 3rd Detachment of Ohio Militia "Blunt's Cunts." They have pitched their tents in a hollow square on the W. side of Central Park. Capt. Blunt checks his soldiers' feet, armpits, rations, weapons, etc., daily. (Capt. Shaffer is a drunkard; 3 of his men, including Sgt. "I'm in Command Here," have deserted within the last 48 hours.)

Constipated. A burning in my stomach.

Dug stumps from Central Park with Lambright & Beam, whose wives almost came to blows arguing about a recipe for turtle soup. Said Hattie,

"We've been cooped up together too long."

Late this afternoon, Otto Fischer returned from Mt. Vernon with his brindled cow—milk for Carrie, who is troubled with gripes.

Constipation relieved (5:30 PM). Bleeding piles.

11:30 PM. Small blue eyes. High cheek bones. Roman nose. The red in her hair. Broad shoulders. The down on her arms.

Need a drink.

6 Oct.

Sold to Capt. Blunt at his HQ, "The Liberty
Tree," Mans., 60 bushels my corn, @ .40 per
bushel, for which I have his receipt-in-hand
promising Gen. Beall to pay me in one month ... $24.00.

Lambright reckons that Gen. Beall already owes us $352.80 for 440 bushels of corn, 5 barrels salt, 30 half barrels flour.

Addressing Blunt: "Is the General good for it? Your men tell me they ain't been paid in a month. Some ain't got shoes or blankets; none was issued an extra shirt or pair of pantaloons."

Blunt: "True."

Bob (behind bar): "What about our $352.80?"

"Gentlemen, I'll be blunt. Shame on you! Talking about money when savage Indians have ravaged you! Why, the British army may march to the Ohio River and take possession of the state.

"What are your sufferings compared with those of your sires in the War of the Revolution? They oft could be traced, when marching to meet the enemy, by the blood oozing from their bare feet on the snow.

"Fellow citizens! Have faith! Soon all crooked things will be made straight. You'll get your $352.80. Mean time, cultivate a spirit of subordination, patriotism and courage, and ere long your dead will be avenged and the recent victory gained by the enemy at Detroit refunded with double interest. The haughty British lion shall be subdued by the talons of the American eagle!"

Lambright (with straight face): "Thanks for being blunt!"

Blunt raised his glass of Port & said, "The enemies of our country! May they make an eternal journey wearing cobweb britches, on porcupine saddles and hard-trotting nags!"

10:30 PM. At Beam's suggestion, I blew tobacco smoke into a gill of water and drank it for my burning stomach—it works!

7 Oct.

Cloudy morn. with no fog or dew; gentle S. wind.

Went hunting with Lambright & Pru, who treed a coon which I shot. We returned Mans. about 1 PM to discover Fanny & Chapman had just arrived on Gen. Wayne.

She sat on the beech stump in the middle of Main St., cried out for Carrie & suckled her, singing,

> Doodle, doodle do.
> The princess lost her shoe.
> The princess hopped,
> The fiddler stopped,
> Not knowing what to do.

Fanny (soaking her feet): "Them redskins gave me lice."

Chapman without his celebrated pasteboard visor. He says Tommy Lyons tortured Jethro Stone to death Mon. night in the former's camp 2 miles S. of the E. shore of Lake Sandusky.

"Ka-ha-suna come to Tommy Lyons in a dream the night after he attacked us at Beam's saying, 'Capture a brave warrior in battle and give him to me at the new moon for a fiery husband.' "

"I says to Tommy Lyons, 'Ka-ha-suna is your Guardian Spirit, thanks to me. You owe me a favor in return.'

"Says he, 'Would you like to eat fire, too?'

" 'Yes,' says I. 'Free my friend, Jethro Stone. Burn me in his stead.'

" 'You know I cannot,' says he. 'You are like a father to me.'

" 'En-kwise,' says I. 'My son. Free the squaw.'

"He smiles—Injuns don't smile much—and says, 'You and the squaw watch your friend die, then go.' "

Fanny: "We did."

After a hot bath & change of clothes, she supped on Hattie Lambright's turtle soup & fell asleep upstairs in the blockhouse about 4 o'clock. Awoke screaming 4 hours later. Hattie gave her 16 drops laudanum in a dram of whisky.

11:30 PM. Chapman, at "The Liberty Tree": Tommy Lyons commands 25 warriors, seven of whom are mounted. All are armed with new British muskets, scalpers & pipe tomahawks supplied to them, along with blankets, powder & shot, from Detroit. Their camp is near a spring among a stand of huge sugar trees. Plentiful deer, turkeys, pheasants; many signs of bear. "The crabapples were ripe."

Snug little shelters behind felled logs facing the NW; scaffolds hung with meat. C. recognized Martha Seymour's scalp dangling by its fair hair from a pole.

"The Injuns dug a pit deep enough for Jethro Stone to stand upright. Then they put him into it, hands tied behind his back, and rammed earth all round his naked body, up to his neck. His head was above ground. Immediately the new moon rose—about 7:30—Tommy Lyons scalped him and there let him remain for three hours.

"Stone screamed, 'Shoot me! Shoot me! Shoot me!' while they danced around him. Then Tommy Lyons made a small fire behind Stone's head and kept it burning two hours till Stone's eyes gushed from their sockets and he died."

8 Oct.

Fanny moaned in her sleep.

"Ma says you watched over me all night, Tom."

"Let's get married right away."

Mrs. Cooper: "Yes, daughter, do. Don't fret about me. Or Sarah. Brother Beam will see us safe to Cincinnati. For that's where I must go. I can't stand it here another minute. Everything reminds me of Henry or Ezra. Marry him, daughter. Sarah and I will make out."

"Oh, Ma!"

"Dry your eyes, daughter. Look at me. I don't hardly cry no more."

"I'll marry you Monday, Tom. On my Pa's birthday. Like we planned."

Over breakfast, she said, "That woman is trying to make me feel bad, Tom. She never called me 'daughter' before!"

Beam & I gathered & burned garbage around the blockhouse. He is unconcerned about 225 mile trip with Sarah & Mrs. Cooper thro' woods to Cincinnati. "I'm going to die of pneumonia in December, like Montour said. God gave that red devil the gift of prophecy to try my faith. I'm sure of it. Pneumonia! A horrible death—drownded in my own phlegm. Oh, God! I fear that I will deny You while I'm dying, and burn in Hell."

Fanny said, "I lost my faith Monday night."

Chapman: "There is no death. Let there be neither sorrow, nor crying. Jethro Stone is now an Angel in Heaven. He wears a shining white linen robe."

Fanny: "Does he have eyes?"

At sunup, Mon., 62 guests will fetch Fanny & then me to Central Park while firing guns, blowing hunting horns, ringing cowbells, banging pots & pans, etc. We will be married by F. M. Eliphalit Austin Jr., Mt. Vernon's Justice of the Peace.

8 PM. Rain. Lambright called roll at blockhouse just so Fanny could cry, "Present and accounted for!" Applause & cheers.

Mrs. Cooper told Fanny, "I can't come to your wedding. Central Park holds too many painful memories for me."

On the march, Fanny noticed ripe crabapples, black haws & elder berries. "I was famished. I went two days on one piece of venison, about the bulk of an egg. My breasts ached the whole time. Jethro watched me squeeze out milk to relieve the pressure and said, 'What a waste, ma'am!'

"Injuns pitch camp after dark with ten or twelve to a fire. They sleep on brush, wrapped in blankets, their feet toward the flames. They kept Jethro with one bunch; me with the other. No blankets. Our hands were tied behind us, about the wrists and above the elbows, all night.

"Tommy Lyons hit Jethro with the pipe end of his pipe tomahawk every chance he got. Jethro said to me,

" 'Remember! No matter what happens, it's better to have lived than not.'

"His nose was bleeding.

"The second night—Sunday—Tommy Lyons trimmed Phil's scalp down to about two inches in diameter. He dashed the scalp in my face.

"I was a slave."

C.: With Ka-ha-suna wed, Tommy Lyons quit these parts. He planned to sell Fanny to Tecumseh, who's camped with about 200 of his Shawanoes on the Detroit River.

9 Oct.
Bought of Delight Coffinberry at Bob's store,
Mans., 2 lbs. pig tail tobacco @ .16...................... .32.
Bought of the above, 6 lead pencils, @ .20......... $1.20.
Bought of the above, 5 sheets of Royal size
drawing paper, @ .03 .... .15.

A passion to draw today. This morn., sketched Lettiece, who was snoring in the corner by the hearth, "The Liberty Tree."

Bob said, "Drunk as a skunk. Fanny bought her a bottle of rum."

Lettiece opened one eye & said, "You can't draw me for free. That will cost you a glass of rum."

Courtesy of the Thomas Keene Collection, Mansfield, Ohio.

"Address me as Massa."

She made a grab for the sketch, which got crumpled & torn at the top.

At 1:30 PM, conceived the idea of making Carrie an alphabet book. Will draw, cut & print by hand 26 wood blocks.

At 2 PM,

Bought of Delight Coffinberry, at Bob's store,
Mans., 1 burning glass .... $1.15.

2–3 PM. Observed a large black ant (Hymenoptera) thro' the above. Drew aforesaid ant encountering the letter A.

Capt. Blunt moved his camp, which became muddy because of last night's heavy rain, to E. side Central Park. Lambright thinks that with three companies of militia here and Tommy Lyons gone, it's safe to return to our cabins. This afternoon, Grace (sober but shaky) & Sam Lewis bought Fischer's brindled cow for $25., & headed home.

Fischer will fiddle at our wedding feast; Lambright my best man, Beam will give Fanny away. Blunt & Shaffer will supply all the game. One of the latter's men cut himself badly on the hand with his tomahawk.

Mrs. Cooper will auction off her corn, land, etc., at her cabin on Tues. morn. & depart by ox cart for Cincinnati with Sarah, Pru & Beam. Sarah still carries around her Pa's powder horn. She said,

"I'm coming to your wedding, Tom. Afterwards, we'll never see each other again. I've liked you since we met— Whitsunday, a year ago. You stuck out your hand to me and said, 'My name's Tom Keene. What's yours?'"

"Grown-ups never introduce themselves to kids. They just ask your name. Not you. I'll miss you, Tom."

11 PM. Fanny: "I hear you got drunk twice in my absence, Tom! I will not marry a drunkard! Give up booze and sell your Still or find another wife!"

Courtesy of the Thomas Keene Collection, Mansfield, Ohio.

11:30 PM.

Sold to Bob Coffinberry at Kratzer's
blockhouse, Mans., one hammered copper
Head, with pewter charging pipe, etc. .... $7.00.
Sold to the above, one hammered copper Still,
well-tinned, of 27½ gall. .... $17.50.
Sold to the above, one set of Maple Worm tubs,
hickory hoops .... 1.50.

10 Oct.

Paid to Lettiece Shipman, in Central Park, to
keep her mouth shut about us........................... $5.00.

"You is the lowest white man yet!"

Chapman & I removed and winnowed 15 bushels of oats
from the upper part of the blockhouse. He told me that he
& Lettiece will spend the winter in Fanny's old cabin. C:

"Lettiece is safe with me. 'For there are eunuchs, which
were so born from their mother's womb; and there are some
eunuchs, which were made eunuchs of men; and there are
eunuchs, which have made themselves eunuchs for the kingdom of heaven's sake.' Matt. 19:12. I am a eunuch for the
kingdom of heaven's sake."

He bought the corner lot on Diamond St. & Park Ave. S.
from Bob at noon for $40.

An hour later, Col. "Dutch" Kratzer & his mounted Mt.
Vernon riflemen—black & dirty as Indians—returned from
escorting the Del. to Upper Piqua. C. broke the news about
Jethro Stone.

Kratzer: Chief Armstrong died of the cholera on the night
of 20 Sept. in Berkshire Twp. His last words: "Au-lute-tau-
o-con-a!" (Avenge me!)

"The Injuns painted his corpse red and cut a hole in his
coffin so his spirit could escape. Silas married his Pa's two
squaws. I took the old man's bay mare."

Central Park is hung with fresh venison, turkeys, a few
ducks.

Fanny's hope chest, given her at "The Liberty Tree," after supper, contains the following:

A blue & white coverlet from Mrs. Cooper & Sarah.
2 cotton sheets from Hattie.
A pattern quilt from Ma Beam.
Table linens from Delight & Grace.
2 feather pillows from Lettiece.

On behalf of the Officers & Men of the 3 Companies of Ohio Militia garrisoned in Mans., Capt. Blunt gave Fanny a 2 gall. cast iron kettle, filled with divers cooking necessities— 2 iron meat hooks, 4 spoons, 4 forks, 1 butcher knife, 2 grease skimmers, a trammel & 1 pint tin cup.

Otto Fischer gave her a wooden trencher.

10:30 PM. Kratzer: "The crazy naked squaw drownded crossing Elm Creek in Delaware County."

11 PM. Fanny: "When I first seen Johnny talking with Tommy Lyons—they was seated on a bearskin—I didn't know what to think. Johnny winked at me. Tommy Lyons puffed on a pipe tomahawk. They talked near two hours. The Injuns fed Jethro and me a little bread made of corn meal, pounded in a hommony block, mixed with boiled beans and baked under ashes.

"Then they stripped Jethro naked, tied his hands behind him, and blackened his face and body with charcoal and water. He sobbed.

"It took one warrior another hour to dig the pit. Jethro watched the sun go down. He said,

" 'When I was a kid, I wanted to go to sea. Can't think now why I didn't.'

"They dropped him into the pit. Tommy Lyons raised a tune. Injuns sing in high voices. They sound like little girls. Tommy Lyons kept time by rattling a small gourd, filled with pebbles or beads.

"Jethro's brains boiled in his head.

"The Injuns sang and danced all night. At daybreak, two

warriors dug up Jethro's body, cut off his arms, legs and head, and stuck them on poles. The Injun dogs ate the rest.

"Help me live without Jesus, Tom."

"I'll do my best."

11 Oct. Sun.

Received in full of John Chapman at my home
this morn., 6 four year old apple trees he owed
me for reading Swedenborg's "Heaven & Hell"
(cf. 31 July, 1811); & 6 more as his wedding
present.

He planted the trees in my orchard. Lambright & I laid puncheons in the new room, cleaned out & daubed chimney, repaired roof, washed ashes from fireplace & floor with lye water, replaced ropes on bed. Bob came by about 3 PM to fetch the Still; remained to lend a hand. He removed the nest some field mice had made of milkweed down in the top drawer of my cupboard.

C: "Tommy Lyons is on the war-path, because I love myself. He was a drunkard and 'ah-lux-soo'—empty, without a Guardian Spirit. I couldn't leave well enough alone and got him Ka-ha-suna. She's crazy. Evil Spirits are crazy."

10 PM.

On My Forthcoming Marriage to Fanny.

Tomorrow, I will start
With thee
A journey on the flood-tide
Of my heart.

Thou art water
Fit to drink,
Fresh bread,
The North
That stopped the arrow
Spinning in my head.

11 PM. *Masturbatus sum* (Fanny).

From "The Mansfield Gazette and Richland Farmer," 31 Mar. 1845:

In Memoriam: John Chapman, late of this town, who died at Age 71 in Fort Wayne, Indiana, on March 10, 1845.

By Lydia Maria Child.

Johnny took apples in pay for chores,
And carefully cut from them the cores.
And journeying thus o'er prairies wide,
He stopped now and then, and his bag untied.

With pointed staff deep holes he would bore
And in ev'ry hole he stuck a core;
Then covered them well, and left them there
In the keeping of sunshine, rain and air.

Sometimes a log cabin came in view,
Where Johnny always found jobs to do.
He had full many a story to tell,
And goodly hymns that he sung right well.

"I once saved a Mansfield maid,
From an Indian's scalping blade.
I could not do the same for one
Jethro Stone, militiaman.

"The redskins scalped and burned his head."
Johnny said, "He ain't dead.
Jethro's Spirit walks with me,
Companion in my misery."

In cities, some said the old man was crazy,
While others said that he was lazy.
But he took no notice of jibes or jeers,
He knew he was working for future years.

So he kept on traveling far and wide,
Till his old limbs failed him, and he died.
He said at the last, " 'Tis a comfort to feel
I've done some good, though not a great deal."

Weary travelers, journeying west,
In the shade of his trees find pleasant rest,
And they often start, with glad surprise,
At the rosy fruit that round them lies.

And if they ask, "Whence came the trees
That drop such luscious fruit as these?"
They learn the answer, traveling on:
"The trees were planted by Appleseed John."

16 July, 1845

Dear Ezra,

Happy birthday! Herewith, unexpurgated, as promised, Vol. 1 of my Journal (1 July 1811–11 Oct. 1812)—how your Ma & I came to wed. She has long since read it and forgiven me.

I tacked on Sissy Child's poem from the Gazette because it prompted me to make my own "In Memoriam—Johnny," a woodcut, which I enclose under separate cover via the Cincinnati stage.

Carrie dined here Mon. & said, "Miles and me are getting along much better since we moved back to town." I didn't believe her, but took Ma's advice. "Don't butt in!"

Again, Happy Birthday!

Kiss Meg & the girls for me. What did Kitty name her pony?

How's your business?

Love,
Pa

Courtesy of the Thomas Keene Collection, Mansfield, Ohio.